high holiday stories

Frederick Fell Publishers, Inc
2131 Hollywood Blvd., Suite 305 • Hollywood, Fl 33020
www.Fellpub.com • email: Fellpub@aol.com

high holiday stories

rosh hashanah & yom kippur thoughts
on family, faith and food

NANCY RIPS

Frederick Fell Publishers, Inc
2131 Hollywood Blvd., Suite 305
Hollywood, Fl 33020

For information about special discounts for bulk purchases. Please contact Frederick Fell Special Sales at business@fellpublishers.com.

Designed by Elena Solis
Manufactured in Canada

10 9 8 7 6 5 4 3 2 1

Library of Congress Cataloging-in-Publication Data
Rips, Nancy.
High holiday stories : Rosh Hashanah & Yom Kippur thoughts on family, faith, and food / Nancy Rips.
    p. cm.
Includes bibliographical references and index.
ISBN 978-0-88391-191-4 (hardcover : alk. paper)
1. High Holidays. 2. Faith (Judaism) 3. Jewish families--Religious life. 4. Food--Religious aspects--Judaism. I. Title.

BM693.H5R57 2010
296.4'31--dc22

                               2010020594

ISBN 13: 978088391-191-4

To Tom,
my one of a kind twin brother

On Rosh Hashanah it is written,
and on Yom Kippur it is sealed

Sure we were chosen, but for what?
It's an honor we could have lived without.

—*Anonymous*

When we really begin a new year it is decided,
And when we actually repent it is determined,
Who shall be truly alive
and who shall merely exist.

Yom Kippur Prayer

contents

introduction

The High Holidays are the most important festivals of the Jewish year. Beginning in the fall with Rosh Hashanah and ending ten days later with Yom Kippur, the Day of Atonement, Jews all over the world observe these historic days.

Rosh Hashanah is known as the New Year, but the only similarity with January 1 is to use it as a day for making resolutions. It's a time to look seriously inward and make plans to improve; while Yom Kippur is a day set aside for repentance, recognizing that we are all accountable for our own deeds. In the ten days in between, one is supposed to apologize to anyone they may have hurt intentionally or unintentionally. It's my busiest ten-day period of the year!

In *High Holiday Stories*, 101 people share their own personal observances and experiences. Some of the contributors are household names, while others are known only to their own families and friends. They recount varied Rosh Hashanah and Yom Kippur experiences—from the Colorado Rockies to Army bases in Iraq, even online in Los Angeles. They describe reuniting for holiday meals and wearing their finest clothes to synagogue. Although their stories are as varied as their personalities and circumstances, all speak to the core values of Judaism—family, faith, and, yes, food.

For me, the High Holidays are a time to connect with the people I love and a time to make amends to those I may have hurt. For my seven-year-old friend, Olivia, Rosh Hashanah is a time for being thankful and asking forgiveness: "I'm supposed to tell people I'm sorry and mean it."

All Jews have memories of past High Holidays. By sharing them, we can revel in our sameness and celebrate our differences.

high holiday
stories

I

it's beginning to look a lot like rosh hashanah

An introduction to the best-remembered,
lovingly recalled High Holidays of long ago

Rosh Hashanah is designed
to get you to wake up
and pay attention,
not only to who you are,
but to who you have been
and who you mean to be.

—*Rabbi Lawrence Kushner*

I loved sitting next to my dad during High Holiday services and playing with the fringes of his tallit. I would braid them, count them, curl them, and roll them around my fingers. It was a comforting feeling to sit there in the enveloped warmth of my dad.

—Nancy Rips

* * *

Every year, before the High Holidays, I observe my traditional pre-New Year customs—wallowing around in nostalgia, remembering past *yontifs*, thinking about people I miss, berating myself over things I might have done differently, etc. You know—all the introspective behaviors typical of many of us at this time of year. And I've also been reliving my Bat Mitzvah.

My Bat Mitzvah was celebrated on a long-ago Shabbat *Shuvah*, the Sabbath that falls between Rosh Hashanah and Yom Kippur. My father was my teacher. He was a rabbi, old-world style, who "specialized" in teaching (at which he was a veritable Pied Piper) and in reading Torah (at which he was uncommonly gifted and skilled). When Poppa read Torah, each *trope*—each musical note—was flawlessly and lovingly chanted. And his dramatic, intelligent interpretation of the text gave listeners goose bumps, even if the listener had zero understanding of Hebrew—which was usually the case.

Poppa tried to instill his passion for the perfect *trope* and his reverence for the Hebrew word in all his students. Generations of young people sat at his feet, tried their best and still mangled many a *munach* in the process. Poppa listened to all of them and said, simply, "Again." His endurance was legendary.

I was a fidgety pupil. The *trope* came easily enough, but the *haftarah* for Shabbat *Shuvah*, full of exhortations to renounce sin, transgression and iniquity and return—*shuvah!*—to God, held little interest for me. I dutifully practiced for my Bat Mitzvah but my delivery was usually hurried and sloppy and Poppa said, "Again" with regularity.

"So what if I make a mistake, Poppa. Who in the congregation will know?"

"If you make a mistake, touchter, you will know," he answered.

I was only twelve and this wisdom was lost on me.

Now, if my father was the consummate teacher, my mother was the quintessential seamstress. And so, of course, she made my Bat Mitzvah dress. I could have worn that dress inside-out, so exquisitely was it lined and finished. No raw edges. No tangled threads. If a seam didn't meet my mother's standards she simply ripped it out and sewed it again. And again.

"Why do you care so much about the inside?" I asked her. "No one is ever going to see the inside."

"A dress may be beautiful on the outside," my mother replied, "but if the inside is not well-made, the dress will soon fall apart. Any good tailor knows that." This wisdom was lost on me, too.

My Bat Mitzvah, as best I can recall, went just fine. Did I make mistakes? I don't remember for sure, but probably yes. What I do know for sure is that the years since that Shabbat *Shuvah* have not been error-free.

And so, this New Year, I will again say *Al Chet* and ask

atonement for my sins. The sins of pride, anger, ingratitude, jealousy, disrespect, laziness, etc. You know. All the sins of which most of us are typically guilty.

And this year I'll remember my Bat Mitzvah and the teachings of my parents. Lessons even more meaningful to my life than the words of my *haftarah*.

I'll remember to take care with my stitches, Ma. I'll try to tie up all those loose ends and neatly finish the seams. Sure, I'd like the outside to be beautiful, but I'll try to give greater attention to the inside. I want this garment—which is me—to wear well, after all, and not fall apart. Not soon, at least.

And yes, Poppa, I'll remember that when I make a mistake, even one that only I am aware of, it's still a mistake. I'll ask to be forgiven, but this forgiveness may be the hardest to get; for it must come not from others but from me, myself.

"Return, Oh Israel, unto the Lord your God," says the *haftarah* for Shabbat *Shuvah*. "Say unto Him, forgive all iniquity and accept that which is good."

We should say that to one another, too. Forgive all iniquity. Accept that which his good in others and in ourselves.

—*Ozzie Nogg*

* * *

When I was a child, I would steal yarmulkes from my grandparent's synagogue on Rosh Hashanah. Then I'd go home and cut them up to make doll clothes.

—*Michael Kors*

* * *

It has been the practice of my synagogue to take a "break" of approximately three hours in the afternoon of Yom Kippur.

Some people may use this time to take a nap. Others may turn on the television or radio, which may not exactly be in keeping with the tone of the day. Some may just listen to their stomachs growl and, hopefully, not cheat.

Many years ago, I decided that I needed an activity that would be commensurate with my understanding of the purpose of the day. I noticed that the trees were beginning to turn into the annual magnificent display of autumn color, the golds, the greens, the reds, and the yellows. Nature enticed me to take a walk.

While walking, I marveled at the beauty and grandeur of God's creation. I wondered what was my place in it? I thought about where I have been and where I might be going. When I returned, I felt totally refreshed. The fast of the body had turned into a feast of the mind and spirit.

I have followed this ritual for more than 30 years. Eventually, others joined me. Now we have a little havurah. They have said to me that they enjoy the natural sights, the companionship, and the depth of the discussion, often involving the themes of Yom Kippur. And, as one friend pointed out, over the years, it has always been, without exception, a beautiful day.

—*Steven J. Riekes*

I always loved family but I hate Rosh Hashanah family dinners. It's a time when you come face to face with your family tree and realize some branches need to be cut.

—*Rene Hicks*

* * *

Yom Kippur is rather inconveniently timed. Just ask any Jewish baseball player. It invariably falls during either the pennant race or the post-season, which poses a dilemma for players with teams that are championship contenders.

In 1934, my grandfather, Hank Greenberg, was the first big leaguer to sit out a game on the Day of Atonement. He was a man for whom baseball was practically a religion, so his was not an easy decision—particularly because the Tigers were in a close race for the American League pennant and he was a fierce competitor.

The deliberation began with Rosh Hashanah. Much to the consternation of many fans, my grandfather initially announced that it was his intention to sit out the Jewish

New Year. But a leading Detroit rabbi, presumably a baseball fan, cleared him to play, citing an obscure passage from the Talmud. As it happened, my grandfather provided the two home runs that allowed the Tigers their 2-1 victory against the Red Sox. The Detroit Free Press applauded his effort by publishing a front-page headline the following day reading, "Happy New Year, Hank"—in Hebrew.

With only days left until Yom Kippur, he would soon be faced with another predicament. Despite the fact that he was not particularly observant, he ultimately decided to sit out. He realized that his choice was bigger than his personal relationship to his religion. It was about doing the right thing by acting as a representative for the Jewish people. For American Jews, who were still only acknowledged as second-class citizens, his was a meaningful decision. While he would not be met by the roar of the stadium crowd, he was greeted with thunderous applause and a standing ovation when he walked into synagogue.

The Tigers lost that outing, in large part due to his absence. One might say, however, that he won a victory for his people by making the statement that their heritage was something in which they could take pride.

In 1965, Sandy Koufax, the next of the great Jewish ballplayers, also observed Yom Kippur, sitting out the first game of the World Series. Like my grandfather, Koufax was admired for his decision, though it would have dire consequences for the Dodgers that day. Don Drysdale, who pitched in his place, had an abysmal outing, giving up seven runs in 2 2/3 innings. As Dodgers manager Walker Alston approached the mound to pull him from the game, Drysdale gave him a sheepish look, saying famously, "Hey, Skip, I bet you wish I was Jewish today, too."

In recent years, Gabe Kapler has been one of the most vocally Jewish athletes in baseball. He has a tattoo of the Star of David on one leg and the words "Never Again," a reference to the Holocaust, on the other. Given his devotion to his heritage, one would think that the decision to sit out Yom Kippur would be a no-brainer for him. Yet, in both 2001 and 2004, when faced with this choice, he decided to play.

Kevin Youkillis, like Kapler, a player for the 2004 Red Sox, did not take the field that day. Unlike my grandfather and Sandy Koufax, however, he did not go to shul but, rather, suited up and sat in the dugout— perhaps a reflection of his ambivalence. He wanted to honor his religious tradition, but it seemed his heart was in the game. That same year, Shawn Green, who had sat out Yom Kippur in 2001, was scheduled to play not one but two games over the holiday. In the end, he went with a compromise, playing one and sitting the other. Green said that, while he was not religious, he felt it was important to at least acknowledge his faith.

When asked about their respective decisions, players have responded that it is a personal choice—that every individual has to do what is right for him.

That is not entirely true.

Heavy though the burden may be, I believe that Jewish players share the same obligation as my grandfather—to serve as representatives for their people. Admittedly, he lived in different times. Jewish athletes, however, still have the ability to affect their communities.

If Kevin Youkillis and Shawn Green had wanted to send a message, they might have been more effective if they had made stronger commitments to their positions. Moreover, since Gabe Kapler cares so deeply about the Holocaust, he could have acknowledged the people who lived through it by exercising a right that they were denied—the right to be Jewish, to observe Yom Kippur.

Ultimately, the decision to sit on Yom Kippur is not necessarily about religion but rather heritage, tradition and pride. If there are any Jewish players left standing come this Yom Kippur, I hope they bear that in mind, remembering that, as Jewish ballplayers, their decisions are bigger than simply personal ones.

—*Melanie Greenberg*

* * *

Rosh Hashanah is one of my favorite holidays. Maybe it's the whole back-to-school thing that never goes away, but for me it really is a New Year. I like taking the time to think about where I'm going.

—*Lois Berman*

Since my mother's death,
High Holiday services have become
profoundly meaningful for me.
It becomes a window, to stop the
wheels of life from turning at a
frenzied speed. And it becomes a time
to contemplate the larger picture of
my own life as a human being,
a citizen of the world, and as a Jew.

—*Peter Yarrow*

My grandparents, Annie and Morris Freedman of blessed memory, lived across the street from the Ahavath Achim Synagogue in Atlanta, Georgia. In the early years when the synagogue moved to this destination, they proudly moved too and bought a brick house directly across the street. The AA, as we called it, is the largest conservative synagogue in Atlanta and their home was a wonderful testimony to their love of the synagogue. Above the mantle place in their den, while a likely object would today be a work of art or a Plasma television, they had an oversized gold key, which was the key to the synagogue. My grandparents bought it in 1920 when they purchased it to help support the synagogue. The key is now part of the Breman Jewish Museum in Atlanta, but it was clearly one of their most prized possessions.

Every holiday was spent enjoying the platters of traditional Jewish foods that my grandmother made. My parents always made sure I had a Rosh Hashanah outfit and new shoes. The food flowed out of my Grandma's tiny kitchen like a constant river stream—tszimes, brisket, the best-baked chicken ever, mashed potatoes. She effortlessly made each and every item including the chopped liver and gefilte fish. The dessert centerpiece waiting for us when we got out of services was always Grandma's platter of sweets, which would have made her world famous today by any standards.

We had a permanent parking place at their house and never had to worry if a cookie and Coca-Cola break was in order. Their house was meticulously kept and there was a basket by the old-style black telephone that was filled with requests for donations to Israel. My generous and devoted grandfather collected for Israeli charities, and to this day my father continues the tradition.

Their house, though small, had room for all of us. Aunts, uncles, cousins, distant cousins, or whoever needed a place to go for the High Holidays. The fine silver, china and starched white tablecloths were pristinely presented. My grandfather led the Hamotzi and the rabbi's sermon was ceremoniously debated throughout the meal. The family cascaded the long dining table, which stretched across two rooms, and I always sat next to my little cousin Steve, with whom I cracked jokes about everything from the silverware to anything we thought was funny.

While our entire family all lived in the same area, we now stretch across Atlanta. Our family splits up so that everyone takes turns being with respective family members of opposite sides. We are blessed with two children now, Ali who is 22 and Justin who is 28. We continue to create traditions for them. We are fortunate that my talented and very loving Aunt Lois who is a fabulous cook hosts the first night, and for years we have spent the holiday with their side of the family with whom we are so close. My beloved four grandparents, Annie and Morris Freedman and Pauline and Irving Blonder, along with my husband's parents, aunts and uncles, and cousins, whose blessed memory reside in our hearts, leave a vacant hole that can never be filled.

The holidays should be a happy time, but for me it's a flashback to a time of simple pleasures, abundant family and pure joy. I miss the certainty of everyone being there, the pineapple cookies, my grandmother proudly welcoming us at the front door after shul in her little apron, and even those platters of roasted chicken.

Someone once said to me, "Today is the simplest day of the rest of your life." I just wish I could go back and have one more of those simple High Holidays with everyone present. Those were the days.

—*Robin Freedman Spizman*

* * *

We were very poor, but I never knew it. I was given a secure upbringing and I always felt loved and wanted. Gramma and Grandpa taught me Jewish traditions and raised me to be polite, caring, and sensitive, a gentleman.

—*Barry Manilow*

I remember Rosh Hashanah and Yom Kippur services at our old Orthodox synagogue. I must have been 9 or 10 years old when I first began wondering why my mother, sister, and I were seated upstairs, and why my father, separated from us, was in a seat downstairs. I was too young to fully understand the laws requiring this positioning, but as time passed I drew my own conclusions. I decided that because my father had to "look up" to see us, and we, in turn, "looked down" on him, we women, must have been the honored ones with the prize seats. I like to believe that to this day.

—Paula Albert

* * *

It's funny, as an adult I'm not a profoundly religious person in an organized way, but after September 11, it was important for me to go to Temple on Rosh Hashanah and Yom Kippur, like my family always did.

—Debra Messing

I was pious once. As an earnest student at a Jewish Day School in Chicago, I took everything to heart. Our closeness. Our holiness. The fact that everyone is made in the image of God. In one classroom, a laminated sign hung permanently on the wall alerting us to the fact that the rabbis said that publicly humiliating someone is akin to murdering them. I made a mental note of that.

Needless to say, I practically grew up in my family's conservative synagogue, where I was a champion Torah reader. Summers meant text and Hebrew classes at a Jewish camp where most Friday evenings you would find me cramming to learn the Torah portion for Shabbat morning. One summer I even learned the troupe for the Song of Songs and chanted it in front of the entire camp on a Friday night, landing me a "certificate" for being the youngest person to read *Shir HaShirim* at Camp Ramah. I proudly hung this certificate on my bedroom wall at home. In short: I wasn't messing around in the Serious Devotion to God Department.

So it comes as no surprise that one Yom Kippur I

undertook the custom to wear all white clothing. After all, white symbolizes purity and on the holiest day of the year; we are supposed to prostrate ourselves before God and atone for our human shortcomings. I was aiming for the transformation promised by the prophet Isaiah when he said, "Though your sins be as scarlet, they shall be as white as snow."

So the "snowy" look was my intention that Yom Kippur when I put on everything white I came across in my closet. The only problem was, as a ten-year-old I had no fashion sense. I actually still don't, but especially then, in adhering to the all-white rule, I failed to recognize that I wore a "winter" off-white wool sweater and a "summer" bright white cotton skirt. On my feet, to avoid the no-leather rule, I wore canvas Keds sneakers, the '80s shoe-wear of choice for Schechter girls. I only know I erred because of my sister's sneakers. Older and fashionably wiser, she was technically in the right. But our mother shushed her, an act of significance from the same woman whose constant refrain is, "Every time you leave the house, you should know that you look good."

In other words, Torah and scholarship trumped fashion. At least on Yom Kippur. It would be a lie to say that I entered adulthood with my piety intact. I did not. Something happened that, while still steeped in Jewish life, observance just never stuck. But at my core, I love supplicating myself to a higher power. And even if I have learned the hard way that good people are not necessarily rewarded, or more importantly, that bad people aren't necessarily punished, deep down I like to believe that there is a right path and a wrong one.

I also haven't worn all white on Yom Kippur since my debut over 20 years ago, but the memory has sparked an idea: Maybe for next Yom Kippur I can try to find a white Diane von Furstenberg wrap dress. With perhaps a small red leaf peeking out to symbolize sin as a driven leaf.

After all, where is it written that purity can't be just one slimming wrap-dress away?

—*Abigail Pickus*

Every year when I was a child,
I went to synagogue on Yom Kippur
with my dad. There was a point in the
service when the entire congregation
would cover their eyes with their hands.
My father told me not to look but I did.
I peeked and I saw these guys with their
raised hands and forked fingers.
I've always said: That's where the
vulcan greeting came from.

—Leonard Nimoy

I grew up in Milwaukee with Orthodox grandparents on both sides. The High Holidays meant visiting them at their Temples. We walked from temple to temple, visited the relatives and then, since we didn't have to attend school that day, went shopping for new shoes.

—Howard Silberg

* * *

W hen my grandchildren were small, I decided that the High Holidays (with all their "fear and dread"), should also be a time of joy. After all, we Jews are welcoming a New Year and a chance to "start over." Thus, when we gather for dinner on Erev Rosh Hashanah, we welcome the evening with music and dancing which begins in a snake-like manner throughout the house and finishes at the dining room table.

I play a CD with joyous music as we begin the dancing, and then we circle the table and seat ourselves. The young people know that we are praying for a year of peace, but more importantly, we share with each other the things which we, as individuals as well as a family, can do to make the world a better place. In so doing, each of us has to admit where he or she has room for improvement in the coming year. Me, too!

—*Phyllis Glazer*

* * *

My dad was very observant and had a beautiful singing voice. In fact, he always wanted to be a Cantor.

—*Cheryl Kricsfeld*

* * *

I grew up in New Haven, Connecticut. At Rosh Hashanah services every single woman wore a mink stole. And the weather had nothing to do with it. I can still see all those minks coming and going!

—*Gloria Kaslow*

I have always considered my Jewishness to be a journey. Maybe that's because as a child it actually took a journey to observe the High Holidays every year.

I grew up in Grand Island, Nebraska, 150 miles west of any large city. Yes, there were Jews in Grand Island—our family as well as a few other families, but it was very important to my parents that my two older sisters and I grew up with a Jewish identity, even though building that identity took time away from our everyday lives and required travel at least twice each year.

Every year on Erev Rosh Hashanah (usually right after lunch), my family would get in the car for our first of two annual pilgrimages to Omaha. We used to spend the night at a hotel. Dinner every Erev Rosh Hashanah and Kol Nidre was at Ross's Steakhouse. While other people savor the smells of kreplach, gefilte fish and brisket, the scents of prime rib with a side of spaghetti take me back a few decades.

After dinner it was time to get to Temple for the late service. Timing was always tricky. You didn't want to arrive too soon or the traffic was impossible as the early service attendees left the parking lot at both Temple and the church across the street. Get there too late and you didn't get the seats you wanted.

After attending Rosh Hashanah morning services, it was back in the car for the journey home, but not without the stop at Bishop's Buffeteria for what this little girl thought was the coolest lunch place on the planet!

This routine was repeated nine days later for Yom Kippur. Was it hard for my parents and our whole family to make this trek twice each year? Yes. Did it inconvenience everyone? Yes. But did my parents' commitment to our Judaism help build my Jewish identity and desire to continue my lifelong Jewish journey? Absolutely! And for that, I am forever grateful to my mom and dad.

—*Sally Zipursky*

I grew up in a small steel mill town in pennsylvania. Most of my high holiday memories are culinary ones, except for my plaid taffeta dress and Mary Jane shoes I wore to services. But to this day, I can still see my mother's golden yellow chicken soup with the fat floating on the top.

—*Darlene Golbitz*

When I grew up, we were the only Jewish family in a small town, and it was painful because I was a frequent victim of anti-Semitism. I was aware of other children who called me bad names because I was Jewish. The worst incident happened in fourth grade. We were supposed to take a two-hour Bible class, but since I was Jewish I did not attend. My teacher felt I should be punished for skipping this class and kept me in the classroom with the lights off, the shades drawn, and the door locked. I was told to put my head down on the desk until the class returned.

I believe my Jewish identity and love of the holidays, especially Rosh Hashanah when my entire family gathers, became stronger because of those abusive incidents.

—*Jan Schneiderman*

* * *

I remember the first Rosh Hashanah service I attended with my Jewish husband. Being a Roman Catholic, I was stunned to see that Jews attend religious services so often and for so long. I wasn't sure what to wear for my first time in synagogue, so I asked my Jewish friend. She advised, "Bring out the major jewels."

—*Julianne Dunn Herzog*

* * *

Being a child of the '30s and '40s was almost idyllic. And no time was happier than Rosh Hashanah was for me. Our family dinners, when we returned from synagogue, were special. Our mother always prepared the most delicious foods: sometimes a roast chicken or a roast duckling made with her special magic seasonings. The table was always set with our best china, silver and crystal. And when I was old enough, I helped my sister, Caryl, with this special assignment.

Some years meant family visits after lunch—family and friends came to our home or we went visiting. Either way, there were wonderful sweets put out, and even though the adults professed to being "too full to eat another bite," the trays of strudel, rugelach, and the other treats both traditional and "modern" were almost empty.

—*Judy Tully*

I always got hand-me-down clothes, except for the High Holidays. But the problem was, my older sister and I got matching outfits; so even though they were new, I had to wear the same dress two years in a row.

—Helen Kay

Over six decades ago I married a girl named Frieda—the most fortunate event in my entire life. She was the most beautiful girl I had ever known and also the very nicest and most loving and caring one as well. We produced four sons and one daughter (who today is an exact replica of her mother). Frieda was without a doubt the most wonderful mother I have ever known. Her children loved her with a love that was deep and never ending. And that love was a two-way street, for Frieda lived for her husband, her children, and her grandchildren. All too soon, she was taken from us but her legacy lives after her in the memories of her family. There has never been one day since that fatal day that I have not missed her in so many ways and I know that this shall be my lot for all the days of my life.

For over forty years Frieda baked one of her challas for each of the Shabbaton we all spent together as a family. As we gathered around the dining table to enjoy the wonders she had chosen to make for us, the place of honor was dedicated to the weekly challah. As the seven of us sang together the Kiddush and the prayer over the wine and the bread, we always finished with the kids taking a piece of the challah and saying, "Mom, this is the best challah you have ever made." And we would all laugh for each one was exactly the same and they were truly wonderful.

As time passed the children all met and married their mates, began to have children, and moved away for one reason or another—usually for the pursuit of a place to earn for their families and to raise them in a special way to the best of their abilities. So it was that when Frieda died, just six months after we celebrated our fiftieth anniversary, I was left all alone and so very sorry for myself, for I had suffered the ultimate loss—the loss of a wife, a lover, a staunch supporter, and a severe critic. Life was indeed an empty, depressing day, one following the other.

So it was that on one of my most depressing of all days that I, feeling especially sorry for myself, spotted her recipe box sitting on the shelf in our kitchen. The thought came to me that perhaps I might be able to find a recipe therein that I could make that might make me feel closer to her even though I knew nothing would or could ever bring her back to me. It was then that I found the recipe for the challah I make today. I read the recipe and although I had never really baked anything (I had always been a reasonable cook but never baked), the question came to me: "I wonder if I could possibly bake her challahs?"

I immediately went to the grocery and purchased all new ingredients—flour, sugar, eggs, yeast, pareve margarine so that it might be eaten with all meals, and came home to try to make one of Frieda's challah. It was a small miracle, for even that very first attempt resulted in the most beautiful challah, one just like Frieda used to make. I was so elated that I called my daughter immediately and told her what had happened. She said, "No Way!" Well, I think it was two weeks later that I made the trip from St. Louis to Kansas City just to show her that I could indeed make Mom's challahs.

About the same time that I learned to make Frieda's challahs, I also found a new House of Worship and that is the story I want to tell now. As you might imagine, I was at a low place in my life having come through the impossible loss of the one person who was indeed my life, my Frieda. I was living in the same condo that we lived in together in

St. Louis and, once again, I was sitting in my den where the two of us had enjoyed our meals together ever since the kids all married and moved away. I was about to have my piece of bagel and cup of coffee when I reached over and turned on the TV. Suddenly, the screen filled with the talking head of a woman with hair that literally filled the entire screen. I was suddenly locked into her presence and her soothing voice as she spoke of the values and the gifts of Judaism. I was suddenly completely engrossed in what she had to say. It seemed as if she was speaking directly to me and what she had to say directly related to my loss. How could this possibly be happening?

When the credits finally came on the screen, they informed me that I had been listening to Rabbi Susan Talve of Central Reform Congregation located in the city of St. Louis, the only synagogue that still resided there since the Jewish population had moved west. Not only that, but they didn't even have a building of their own and had to conduct services in a Unitarian Church. Next came the phone number and times when one might call and find someone there. This all occurred on a Saturday morning, and I jotted the phone number down and vowed to call on Monday morning.

I must digress for a moment to tell you one additional story of grief that had come into our lives just six months following Frieda's death. My daughter's youngest daughter had been struck by lightning while playing in a soccer game for her school against a rival school. It was an overcast day and there was light rain but not a single indication that violent weather was even remotely possible. Suddenly, a bolt was unleashed from above that struck the field where both teams were involved in the game and the force of that bolt knocked all of the children to the ground, but only Katie did not get up. She was revived by two women who did not even know each other but who rushed out to her and performed a miracle as they worked over her. 911 brought medical help finally to awaken her with absolutely no short-term memory. It has been eleven years this past March 30th and to this day she still has no short-term memory.

So it was that with this terrible event coming just six months after the loss of my Frieda that I went to my first Shabbat service at Central Reform Congregation. At the time designated for the prayer for the sick, Rabbi Susan, having read the long list of names that the congregation was already praying for, asked for additional names of those who needed their prayers. I looked around and saw a number of individuals rise, and as Rabbi Susan nodded to each in turn, they all spoke out the names of those who were in need. Finally she nodded to me who had also risen and I stated simply, "My granddaughter, Katie Zemel." She nodded to me and went on to finish the service at which time she came directly over to me and asked, "What in the world is the matter with your granddaughter?" When I had given her a short version of the story, she said very compassionately, "Oh my, we will mention Katie Zemel from this pulpit each Shabbat from now until you tell us that she is on the road to recovery." I was so moved by her compassion that I knew I had to come from then on. Over the next few years she not only became my Rabbi but also my very best and dearest friend.

Three years later we had built a building on the lot across the street from the Church and we were on the way to becoming a very large synagogue. It was on the event of our first "Scholar in Residence" weekend in our new building that I volunteered to cater the five meals needed for the event. I solicited people, and together we provided all the meals for 175 people and did it successfully. Over the next year I introduced Shabbat dinners as well as the first ever Second Night Seder for the congregation, providing all of the food for all of these events. At 76 years of age, I had become a full-service caterer and it was this that once again brought Rabbi Susan to me with a problem.

I was in the office one day and Susan came out of her office and when she saw me she came directly to me and said as follows: "Ray, we buy our challahs each week from this bakery and they are terrible! Not only that but they have the holy chutzpah to charge us $15 to deliver them!" She then cocked her head to one side and said quietly, "Do you think we could make challahs here in our kitchen?" Now, she did not know that I had learned to bake Frieda's challahs, and so I had to tell her how that came about and ended by telling her, "Of course we can make Frieda's challahs in the kitchen." Now the only mixer we owned was a small 5-quart Kitchen Aid home mixer, and I could only make a total of four challahs at a time, so that is what I began with. We used one for Friday night and one for Saturday morning and the other two were snapped up before they had a chance to cool.

It was four or five weeks later that once again Susan came to me and asked, "Ray, Frieda's challahs are the very best but do you think we could make more?" I explained to her the limitations of the mixer we had and that I would need a commercial 32-quart one, on which I would be able to make 16 at a time. Her answer was, "I'll buy it." I told her I would check into the cost and perhaps there was a good used one. Then we could talk. After a bit of networking, I found a perfect used mixer, one for $1,000. I also knew that at my prodding we had established a kitchen fund, so I went to the administrator and told him the story. He asked me, "How much is the mixer you have found?" When I told him he advised me that we had that much in the fund and to go ahead and buy it. I did so and for the first few weeks I made the 16 and we used one on Friday and one on Saturday and we sold the balance for $5 each.

A few weeks later, we found one volunteer and we made 32. Then we found another helper and we made 48, and then we found a third volunteer and we made 64, and the fundraiser was born. At the rate of 64 per week for 50 weeks per year (that allowed for the two weeks of Passover when we could not bake) we would make 3,200 of Frieda's challahs each year and would net a gross of over $15,000 per year. Not a bad few dollars for something that was a love of my life. I could never have made enough money in my entire life to create a memory for the love of my life of that magnitude.

When the time came for me to move on to Kansas City, to be nearer to my daughter, I had only one concern: what would I do to keep busy? Well—and this part you could not know if I don't tell you,—my daughter is one of the leading Kosher Caterers in Kansas City, and she founded the preschool at Congregation Beth Shalom as well as the Senior Center at the Jewish Community Center in Kansas City where they were interested in Frieda's challahs. So I made the move on October 1, 2007, and began to immediately make "Frieda's Heavenly Challahs." I have since traded the Senior Center for the preschool at Temple B'nai Jehudah and am currently making between 80 and 100 challah each week.

While still in St. Louis, we made our first round High Holiday challah for orders we had in house prior to beginning. We offered plain round ones at $5 each and ones with white raisins for $6 each. From the time we began, we had orders for over 200, and it was a huge success. For my first High Holidays in Kansas City, we repeated the process with the result of over 300, also almost equally divided between plain and raisin. For me it is such a wonderful experience to be putting a bit of Frieda into so many homes for the High Holidays.

I am now 86 years of age and am finding that this is absolutely the very best way to grow older. I am busy and productive and doing the one thing that makes me happy. I love sharing the memory of the best person to ever come into my life with so many others. It is important to also add here that the volunteers who have joined me in doing this holy work have been such a god-send as well. They have become my friends and have extended invitations to join them at Shabbat dinners in their homes where I have learned to know and to love them and their families. Even more importantly, they have come to know Frieda through my eyes!

—*Ray Davidson*

Ray Davidson is the kindest, wisest, most sensitive, thoughtful person I know. He enriches everyone's lives of those who get to know him. He now makes challahs every week for our preschool to sell as a fund raiser. He is the first one in the parking lot waiting to be let in so he can start mixing dough. It is so clear that every challah is made with love and beautiful memories of Ray's precious Frieda! Ray said he worked for 40 years and now this is his holy work, both for challah making as well as touching lives. Beth Shalom and I are so blessed to have Ray Davidson in our presence!

—Judy Jacks Berman

ב

why are these holidays different from all other holidays

A potpourri of High Holiday Stories with a twist —on an Army base in Iraq, in Texas after Hurricane Ike, even online in L.A.

Who knew Yom Kippur services were now online in L.A.? The www.jewishtvnetwork.com broadcasts a two-hour Kol Nidre service every year. The goal is to attract Jews who are not affiliated or unable to attend for whatever reason. I know the idea is for Jews to pray with and in a community, but this is an excellent alternative for many: those serving in the military, the disabled, the incarcerated, even those who are alienated from family or synagogues.

—*Nancy Rips*

Last year for Rosh Hashanah, I took a helicopter flight with a Sergeant from Camp Taji to Baghdad, about a ten-minute ride. In Bagdad we were met at the helipad by Rabbi Schranz, a Navy [Cdr] Chaplain. Rabbi Schranz took us over to billeting, where we checked in and assigned a cot in a large air-conditioned tent within walking distance of the mess hall, Post Exchange and Internet café, about three-quarters of a mile from where the services were held in one of the base chapels.

One of the congregants made a handmade Ark for the Torah. We had candles, a Kiddush cup, prayer books, challah, apples, and honey. What more could we ask for? After services Friday night, we made Kiddush and had some challah with honey. Then about 14 of us went to dinner together in the Army mess hall.

First day Yom Tov services began at 9:00 a.m. We went through the Shacharit service, and yes, we marched our Torah around the Chapel. It was quite a sight and very enjoyable! The Rabbi read the Torah, we gave out the aliyahs, and the Rabbi reminded us how lucky we were to get an aliyah on Yom Tov for free! Our grandparents had to pay for the honor of an aliyah in their old shuls. I had the third aliyah. It was quite an honor. I was very proud that my father's name was mentioned in an aliyah in Baghdad, Iraq, for Rosh Hashanah.

We all had kosher MRE's (Meal, Ready to Eat—the Army's field rations) for lunch. Mine was a Kosher-for-Passover MRE, with a can of salmon, some raisins, cranberries, and walnuts. We had three beautiful, delicious challahs supplied by the mess hall. There is a Filipino man there who makes them for Friday night services every week. And the Rabbi poured Kedem and Rashi wine for Kiddush.

Second day Yom Tov, it was pretty much the same thing. Both days the Rabbi gave inspiring sermons. Almost all of the service was either reading or singing with the Rabbi, responsive readings, and congregant readings. Other than the Rabbi reading Torah, almost everything else involved all of us together. It was one of the most personal and moving services I have ever attended, partly because of where we were, right in the heart of Baghdad. Here were 14

Jews who came together to ensure Rosh Hashanah was celebrated as they always had celebrated it, even though we were in a combat zone.

When the Rabbi said this would be a Rosh Hashanah service we would always remember, I knew he was right. Although we were not in imminent danger, we had Military Police guarding the chapel during our services as a safety precaution. Right in the middle of services, we heard the loud booms of Improvised Explosive Devices (roadside bombs) going off in the distance. On the second day, we heard 15 big booms from some artillery rounds being shot at the bad guys. The chapel shook with each artillery round that was fired, but we just kept on going like it was thunder from a rain shower.

After services the Rabbi took us back to the helipad for our return flight to Camp Taji. It was quite an experience. I wished I would have been home for the High Holidays, but the Army and the Rabbi went out of their way to make them as nice as possible under the circumstances.

—*Captain Jason Rubin*

Some people think because we are English, when it comes to the High Holidays we would approach this time with a certain amount of British reserve. However, the opposite is true. The only use of the word "reserve" that can be applied is to "reserve" extra tables, extra chairs, and, of course, extra waitresses.

Even the most reluctant hostess from England or Wales, while trying out new honey cake recipes (we recommend our *Jewish Princess Cookbook*) will eventually use her Princess Prerogative to call the caterer. That is especially if she finds that her cousins, whom she hardly ever speaks to, suddenly arrive to stay.

—*George Tarn*

and Tracy Fine

During Rosh Hashanah services
when I was a child, my grandpa
Harry used to turn around and
make all the children laugh
by sticking out his false teeth.
My cousins and I would be
hysterical with giggles.
We got in trouble every year.
Grandpa Harry, however, always
turned back around in his seat
and looked totally innocent.

—*Patty Nogg*

As a rabbi in Milan, I was stunned to learn that for Italian Jews, the night before Rosh Hashanah did not include a synagogue service. Instead it was a Rosh Hashanah Seder.

From North to South, from the "thigh" of the Italian "boot" all the way down to the "toe", Italian Jews gather round the family table, and just as we do at Passover, at the Rosh Hashanah Seder, Italians share symbolic foods, blessings, stories, poems, and songs to welcome the New Year.

"*Ricorda, Rabbina,* Remember, Rabbi,' my school director Eva explained. "It's the birthday party of the world. The Rosh Hashanah Seder is our way to have a birthday party." And what a celebration it is! The Seder itself offers an array of foods that symbolize our hopes and dreams for the coming year. Seven bowls are arranged in a circle on the table, much like the Passover Seder plate, but using dates, pomegranates, apples and honey, string beans, pumpkin, spinach, and scallions. Traditionalists place a fish head or a sheep's head in the center of the plate. We modernists choose a head of lettuce instead! Then each bowl is passed around and every guest samples its contents while the Seder leader makes a specific blessing over each food.

The Seder concludes with the passing of the lettuce and the prayer that says, "May it be your will, Oh God, that we be heads, not tails, leaders, not followers. May we always be at the head of what is right and what is good in the year to come."

—*Rabbi Barbara Aiello*

* * *

As a new student at Southern Illinois University and a regular High Holiday attendee, I sought out the High Holiday schedule from Hillel. Walking into the ballroom of the student union, I was shocked by how many students were present. The services were not memorable, but the offer the Rabbi made after services was intriguing. He asked for a few volunteers to join him on the second day of Rosh Hashanah to help make a minyan and help in the service at the Federal Prison in the next town. Always eager to make a minyan, I jumped at the opportunity to meet Jews in jail. Growing up semi-sheltered, I did not know Jews ever ended up in jail.

At the conclusion of services on the second day of Rosh Hashanah, we jumped in the Rabbi's car and headed to the prison. On the way he mentioned that he sent our names in ahead for clearance and that we were okay to enter the prison but not sure if we would be allowed to leave (a little Rabbi humor). He also told us (there was one other student besides me) that this prison is a maximum security prison, and they don't allow visitors during non-visiting times. But since this is for religious purposes they would make an exception.

We arrived and when we passed through the first gate we went through a metal detector and received an invisible infrared stamp on our hands. The guard said that we would not be able to leave if we didn't have the stamp on our hands. We were instructed what to do if there was an "emergency." We went through several other steel-gated passages and into the chapel.

This was in the late '70s, and the clothing style many students wore at that time came from Army surplus stores. I often wore my green Army pants. Well, on this day of Rosh Hashanah I had worn my green Army pants (not sure why), but when we entered the prison I noticed that all of the inmates had on the same pants. I got a little nervous (at least I had on a nicer shirt). I was afraid the guards would mistake me for an inmate.

We weren't in the prison chapel very long and prisoners started to come in. There were only eight prisoners (we later learned there were a few other Jewish inmates but they were not allowed to be with visitors like us) and with the three of us we made a minyan. The prisoners were only allowed an hour for services so we conducted an abbreviated one. Following the service we had time for a Kiddush.

The prison kitchen baked a honey cake, and we had apples and honey. We all sat around and introduced ourselves. Our conversations were pretty typical except for the guy sitting next to me who filled me in on the "truth" of each of the inmates while they told us why they were in prison. They all said they were innocent. He concluded by explaining that "we are all guilty and we are all good liars. We just came for the honey cake and conversation."

—*Alan Potash*

* * *

I have spent several High Holiday seasons on the open seas, including trips to Alaska. On some Cunard ships, more than 100 people attend Rosh Hashanah and Yom Kippur services. It's not a real holiday atmosphere, but many people prefer to leave home and the stress of holidays behind.

Usually one associates the seas with fish, but one year it was a different animal that gave me my most memorable cruising story. A woman walked into the service with a seeing-eye dog. After my sermon, the dog who was trained never to leave his owner's side, jumped up, ran over to me, and put his paws on my shoulder and licked my face. It was the warmest reception of any sermon I had ever given!

—*Rabbi Bernie Lipnick*

I have spent the High Holidays in many different parts of the world. One year I spent Rosh Hashanah on the Siberian Express and on Yom Kippur Eve we were in Kobe, Japan.

In 1970 my mother and I were in Lucerne and the Rosh Hashanah services were held in a ballroom. The Rabbi gave a wonderful sermon in German. And for Yom Kippur that year, we attended a beautiful old synagogue in Vienna. It was quite Orthodox. The women, dressed in their best finery, were seated in the balcony. They paid no attention to the services, but gossiped the whole time!

—Hannie Wolf

* * *

The State of Texas' oldest Jewish congregation, formed in 1850, was forced to usher in the New Year outdoors in 2008. It happened after Hurricane Ike caused flooding and power-outages to its synagogue building. Like much of the island, both Galveston synagogues, Temple B'nai Israel and Beth Jacob synagogue, still were without electricity and plumbing more than two weeks after the storm.

An island of hope emerged in the largely devastated city of Galveston, as 110 local Jews congregated on the back patio of Temple B'nai Israel for a spirited and uplifting community rebuilding Rosh Hashanah service.

B'nai Israel, a Reform synagogue, is home to 180 member households, serving two-thirds of Galveston's Jewish community. The other synagogue, Beth Jacob, a Conservative congregation, did not host High Holiday services this year, after its building suffered heavy damage by the storm.

With sun blazing overhead, and mosquitoes feasting below, B'nai Israel Rabbi Jimmy Kessler held an abbreviated Rosh Hashanah worship service, which included Torah reading and the blowing of the shofar. Music was provided via battery-powered karaoke machine, perched next to a folding card table. This supported a Torah scroll that had been protected in a watertight container during the hurricane. Narrow rows of chairs were laid out in partially shaded areas along the patio.

Some B'nai Israel congregants turned out for the service wearing slacks, neckties and dresses. Many, however, followed the Rabbi's lead and showed up in shirtsleeves and shorts. Most slathered on sun block and insect repellent shortly before the service began at 10:30 a.m. and swapped kippot for broad-brimmed hats and dark sunglasses.

The shofar blowing, in particular, was a poignant part of the service. Rabbi Kessler sounded one shofar from the front, while simultaneously congregant Steve Feldman sounded a second shofar from the back of the patio. The horns' blasts echoed around the surrounding neighborhood, still largely devoid of life.

An Oneg, consisting of bottled water, Oreo cookies and donated challahs, gave the Jewish islanders, many of whom were dispersed after Hurricane Ike, an opportunity to reconnect.

Randy Goldblum has been a B'nai Israel member for 30 years. Planning to stay on the island, he turned out for the Rosh Hashanah service "to keep the tradition going".

Visiting with Goldblum was another longtime congregant and islander, Victor Sierpina. "I came today," he remarked, "because I felt it was important to have a new beginning and an ending."

Sierpina quoted from Tehillah 124: "If the Lord had not been beside us, the torrent would have carried us away, the flood would have washed over us"—saying that these words were "our sustenance during Hurricane Ike." Like Goldblum, Sierpina noted that the congregation greatly needed a place to regroup and find comfort, and that place was at the synagogue that morning on Rosh Hashanah.

Husband and wife, Dr. Armond and Barbara Goldman, have lived on and near Galveston Island for the past 60 years. The Goldmans made the trip to the Rosh Hashanah service from the mainland to support Rabbi Kessler and to see his wife, Shelley, a former classmate of Barbara's.

"We also thought it was important to show support for the community here, not just for the Jewish community, but for the Galveston community, at large," Dr. Goldman said. "Having gatherings like this will help the island come back, we hope."

Immediately after the storm, Debbie Shabot said she was planning to ignore Rosh Hashanah and not celebrate the Jewish New Year, given all the hardships she and her family have endured after Hurricane Ike. "But then, at the last minute, I decided that it would be good to be part of the community. And I'm glad that I changed my mind, because you can see how much community there is here today, people who have lived on the island their whole lives, and newcomers, as well," she observed.

A recent transplant from New York commented: "I've only been here since February, but I thought it was important to be here today to support the synagogue and ensure its future."

Most attendees at the Rosh Hashanah service were B'nai Israel members; however, the congregation also hosted a few guests. One of those guests was Red Cross aid worker Harris Bookfor, a resident of Plymouth Meeting, Pennsylvania, a Philadelphia suburb, who had been working in Red Cross shelters in League City since September 19.

"I've actually been living in a church the past two weeks," Bookfor pointed out. "I really wanted, and needed, to connect with the Jewish community down here.

"Back home, my wife surfed the internet and learned that there was going to be a Rosh Hashanah service in Galveston. I'm Conservative, and am very active with my shul back home, Beth Tikvah/B'nai Jeshurun, but I thought this was the best place for me to go. And, I'm very grateful that the Rabbi and congregation have welcomed me in," he added.

Rosh Hashanah was Bookfor's first day off in ten days. He was scheduled to return to League City for another week of work, and then go home to Pennsylvania.

I took Bookfor to see Beth Jacob Synagogue after the Rosh Hashanah service. In the back, one of the large air conditioning units, which had been compromised by floodwaters, was "crackling" and smelling like wires were short-circuiting inside. Fortuitously, the two were able to shut off the nearby circuit breakers, averting a possible fire, as partial power was being restored to the building.

Galveston will come back and the Jewish community will be an important part of the rebuilding, as we have been in the past. Those of us who are staying on the island are hopeful, as Jews have been throughout our long history, as we begin the New Year.

—*Michael C. Duke*

Volunteering at a nursing home for Rosh Hashanah and Yom Kippur brings a different sort of feeling and memory. I know that for some it will be their very last High Holiday observance. Since many are above 80, they remember the traditional melodies and spiritual feelings of their youth, when they were in their family shul, temple or synagogue for the High Holidays. I try to re-create that feeling with the melodies and prayers, so a connection can be made. Many are joined by their grown children and share those experiences and memories. There is an extra special feeling when everyone sings together and reads responsively, even those who struggle with speech or attention. I am told several times during the year, after a person passes away, how much the service meant to them.

—Andy Greenberg

for years I struggled with my own sense of disengagement at services. I found the prayers overly repetitive.

Everything changed for me during the High Holidays of 2006, the first time since my Bar Mitzvah, 64 years before, that I enjoyed and was moved by a service. The previous November I had sat down with Dana Raucher, the Executive Director of The Samuel Bronfman Foundation, and with Rabbi Darren Levine, Executive Director of the Jewish Community Project, a dynamic new community in lower Manhattan. I poured my heart out, describing the services I had attended and how boring and repetitive they seemed to me. I went on to describe in broad terms that which I wanted: a service full of music and discussion, where one could learn about the history and structure of the service and where study of text was as central as prayer.

What a joy it was to find that Levine, too, had wanted to create such a service and he did, beautifully. In a public room in my apartment building, some 85 people gathered, including family, friends, and many alumni of the Bronfman Youth Fellowships in Israel. Levine, who is over six feet tall, sat on a high stool. With him was a *chazzan* (cantor),

Daniel Leanse, who chanted the prayers and played the guitar, with the backing of a classical cellist and a piano player. The sound was superb. Levine explained the cycle of the Jewish year, showing the congregation that the Days of Awe really start at the beginning of Elul, the month leading up to Rosh Hashanah. Each prayer's significance was explained. There was a prayer for Israel but no sermon.

Kol Nidre and Yom Kippur services followed the same beautiful path. On Yom Kippur morning we had a learning session as we did on Rosh Hashanah, with plenty of participation by the congregants. We broke up at close to 1:00 p.m. then reconvened at 3:00 p.m. for a lively study session on Maimonides' listing of sins. At last my High Holiday prayers were rich in spirituality and learning, in both emotional connection and intellectual engagement. If creative, spiritual, intellectually engaged services like this one were more broadly available, it would no longer be such a struggle for young people to understand the joy in Judaism, a joy that classic sources tell us is fundamental to our religion. "The authentic spirit of Torah is experienced only through gladness," says one Midrash.

—*Edgar Bronfman*

My wonderful grandparents in Far Rockaway, Queens, rarely argued throughout the year. However, you could set a clock to their yearly Yom Kippur blowout. It would happen when Grandpa would walk home from Shul for a short break in the middle of the afternoon. The fireworks would fly! Probably because their Shabbat helper started preparing Break-the-Fast foods and the wonderful smells drove them both nuts! Miraculously once the sun set and the fast was broken they were lovey dovey again—at least till next year!

—*Danielle Gordman*

Like thousands of Jews,
my husband and I mark
the beginning of Yom Kippur,
the Jewish Day of Atonement.
But unlike most worshippers
we do not attend Temple in person.
Instead, my husband, who suffers
from Alzheimer's disease, and I stay
in the living room of our Florida
apartment and listen to the service
on the radio at 8 p.m.

—Florence Greenfeld

I'm the High Holiday pianist for Temple Sinai in Toronto. Being a pianist for one of Canada's largest congregations (5,000+) requires a thorough knowledge of the Rosh Hashanah, Kol Nidre, and Yom Kippur liturgy, as well as sight-reading, transposition, and keyboard harmony skills, not to mention endurance. Because of the size of the congregation, there are two sanctuaries in use. I play in the New Hall for the mostly voice and piano services. Preparation has been much easier this year as a second full-time cantor was hired, who has been a pleasure to work with. His residence means I no longer have to frantically rehearse 3-4 hours of music in, well, 3-4 hours but can spread out rehearsals over several weeks.

—Chris Foley

"Good things come to those who wait." So, I waited and waited for 35 years to abdicate the rabbinate. For the first time, I will spend the High Holidays with my family, not having to worry about my sermons or whether the cantor would take too long singing this-or-that arcane prayer.

After all those years, I will finally have the time and energy to prepare my own gourmet holiday feasts. Whether they are delicious or not, my family and friends will have to feed my fragile ego by telling me that they were "marvelous," and once again, I will have to beat my chest for the sin of arrogance.

But how many years did I spend in other people's dining rooms futilely trying to ingest High Holiday dinners that we would universally declare torturous?

Have any of you had gritty gefilte fish balls? No, not gritty from too much matzo meal, but gritty because they were riddled with shrapnel of fish bones that the lady of the house was either too lazy or too cruel to remove.

While we are on the subject of appetizers, how could I not forget walking with a congregant to his house for lunch on Rosh Hashanah? He prated on and on about his wife's cooking, every superlative synonym, as if he'd swallowed Roget's for breakfast.

Well, you say? You've probably already figured out the rest of the story, but not the magnitude of its horror. Each place was set with a reddish-brown lump atop the customary leaf of lettuce. After the grace, the congregant insisted, "Go ahead, try it."

I tried. The liver oozed blood. Rare chopped liver. The prospects of chug-a-lugging liver blood and contracting E.-coli ran neck-and-neck in my imagination. Then, an atypical stroke of genius: I reached under the table with my fork and stabbed my hands and arms with the tines. Reaching up, I asked the hausfrau what kind of oil she used.

"Canola."

"Canola?" I shrieked. "You can't imagine how allergic I am to canola," and displayed the horrible "rash" on my arm. Beware of rare chopped liver, and keep your fork nearby.

And what do you eat before Yom Kippur, the Great Fast of Atonement? Scientists have debated the issue, but none of them has found anything yet to prevent my backache. Besides, isn't rotten the way we're supposed to feel on Yom Kippur?

One eve of Yom Kippur dinner was particularly memorable. To set the backdrop, the hosts had a huge parrot that kept screaming, "Elliot!" throughout the meal. The lady of the house preceded the main course with a chicken soup that shimmered with a layer of fat so thick and shiny that women were furtively checking their hairdos in it. Not to be outdone, the turkey was so hairy that it begged fitting as a toupee.

Then there was another Yom Kippur eve trying to go into the fast on a dinner of Fruit Loops Chicken. Someone must have thought that it was the culinary equivalent of A+B=C. Sweet chicken tastes good. Breaded chicken tastes good. Therefore, Fruit Loops Chicken must taste good. Maybe in your world. In my world, it's one of those "funny recipes from kids" on Leno. How about chocolate-dipped herring?

A girlfriend once took me home on Rosh Hashanah to meet the family. The aroma of holiday dinner wafted from her aunt's kitchen. A beautiful table was set with honey, apples and round holiday bread.

I recited the Kiddush over wine. They were impressed. They presented the appetizer. Hmm. It was too smooth to be gefilte fish. And besides, it was pink. I tentatively tasted it. "This is delicious," I said to the host. "What is it?"

It's crabmeat salad. It's our tradition to eat it on the first night of Rosh Hashanah."

Crab, you must know, is not merely un-kosher, but super-mega-ultra-un-kosher, right there in Leviticus and Deuteronomy, under penalty of death by stoning or whatever.

Fortunately, the dog ate it ravenously. Afterward, I asked my girlfriend if there were any other family secrets that I should know about. I made it plain that crabmeat salad even once a year was a deal breaker. Then I told her that if we were to go any further, I would happily dye the gefilte fish pink.

Ah, now on to High Holidays with my family, where, "marvelous" or not, at least the liver will be well broiled and the gefilte fish will be kosher.

—*Rabbi Marc Wilson*

3

who put the rush in rosh hashanah

*From a shofar-driven family to preparing festive meals,
it's easy to overlook the traditions and the stories
that give the holidays meaning.*

Rosh Hashanah begins
with its blasts of the shofar
meant to awaken our slumbering
souls to time's passage, and to
what we have done, and more
important, what we can do with
our lives. The new year gives us a
chance to reshape our lives in a
better image by reminding us of
our humanity and our
relationship to god.

—*Michael Strassfeld*

Although the sounding of the shofar on Rosh Hashanah is observed because it is a decree of the Torah, still it has a deep meaning, as if saying: "Wake up from your deep sleep, you who are fast asleep. Search your deeds and repent. Remember your creator, examine your souls, mend your ways and deeds. Let everyone give up his evil ways and bad plans."

—*Moses Maimonides*

* * *

When I was a child, I loved the melodies of the High Holiday services and carefully watched the Cantor sing. When he would turn around, to encourage the congregation to join with him, I thought he was looking directly at me. I was convinced he wanted to help me improve my vocal skills. I would go home and practice singing Ma-Tovu and Ayn Kelohenu in front of my bedroom mirror, with actions.

—*Nancy Rips*

During the month before Rosh Hashanah my mom calls me every day to blow the shofar over the phone! She explains that's the way to get us ready for the High Holidays. I have always been taught that the shofar was meant to be a kind of alarm that roused us from our normal lives and instructed us to prepare for the New Year and the Days of Awe.

—*Micaela Hellma-Tincher*

* * *

Every year at our synagogue, we say, "Time to make and blow your own horn at the hands on, lips on, Shofar Workshop." Politicians have been blowing their own horns long enough lately.

—*Rabbi Shneur Cadaner*

Every year before the High Holidays, I bustle around my kitchen, preparing for Rosh Hashanah dinner. There's a big pot of matzah ball soup, a pan of noodle kugel, honey cake, challah and other traditional Jewish foods. We'll dip our apples and challah in honey so that our year should be sweet.

It's a time for family, but it's also a time for introspection. It's about looking back at all that's happened to us the past year —mistakes I may have made, things I hope to improve.

Some say these High Holidays, from Rosh Hashanah to Yom Kippur, set the tone for the year to come. You're "inscribed" in the Book of Life, for good and bad. Others believe it's how you finish your year that counts the most.

While both are important, for me, what really matters is the moment we're in now, how we choose to spend it, where our thoughts are. That's my challenge every year: to be there, in each moment, as much as possible.

—*Mindy Rubenstein*

As we sat down to Rosh Hashanah dinner each year, our two young daughters would look at each other, and in a private glance, leap up out of their chairs and run outside. Upon their return, they each had a leaf in their hands. They would say, "We are turning over a new leaf as this New Year begins!" Then they would hang their leaves on the refrigerator as a constant reminder of what the New Year could bring to all of us. The leaves would stay there for months, until they were so dry and brittle that they'd fall down.

As the years have passed and the girls have their own families, now I send them a "leaf something" as part of their New Year wishes!

—*Ann Goldstein*

In St. Louis, we have a family dynasty of shofar players. Seven members and three generations of my family, the Lowensteins, go up to the bima every year on Rosh Hashanah and Yom Kippur to blow the shofar in unison.

I began my journey as a shofar player when I was 10 years old. I was given the honor of playing for the Junior Congregation in the small chapel. Shofar blowing came with the genes. My great-uncle, Arnold Weiss, sounded the shofar for my Temple decades before. Then my dad, Erwin Lowensetein, became the shofar player for many years. He gave me tips and showed me how to hold it to my lips. Never did I dream that 63 years later, I would still be doing it, accompanied by my four sons, one daughter, and many grandchildren. And not only do we perform on the High Holidays, we also participate in a community service at the historic new Mt. Sinai cemetery between Rosh Hashanah and Yom Kippur.

I don't know of any other synagogue that has seven family members sounding the shofar. My mom was so proud of this fact that she wrote to the *Guinness Book of*

World Record. They responded, "Thank you for the inquiry, but there's no category for shofar blowers." There should be. As a result, instead of getting in the record books, she made cloth holders with pockets for all the shofars with each blower's name embroidered on a pocket.

My family and I are traditionalists when it comes to Judaism. We're proud to be the shofar-driven family.

—*Robert Lowenstein*

* * *

The shofar needs to be the highlight of the High Holiday service. Jews are required to hear it, and it should provide a profound religious experience because it has been a part of our heritage for thousands of years.

Since I have a background of playing the French horn, one day I called our beloved ritual director, Rabbi Alexander Katz, and asked if I could come "audition" for him. He was most gracious and invited me to his home so he and his wife could hear my attempt. Apparently he was satisfied because for the last 40 years I have been the Ba-al

Tekiah at my synagogue. I vividly remember the last year Rabbi Katz heard me. This wonderful man looked at me, smiled, left his seat, and came over and hugged me. I'm honored to have made this impact on him and so many people in my synagogue.

—*Jerry Gordman*

* * *

Everyone brags about their bubbe's baking, but it was true that my Granny Katie excelled in the culinary department. She had to. After coming from Poland as an orphan, she met my grandfather and had to settle down to raising a family. They eked out a living from my father working as a shoe salesclerk. Money was tight. I remember my dad telling me the story of putting the few coins he earned into a special bank in the wall of their small apartment—only to learn later that it was not a bank but the gas company meter.

—*Rabbi Eliot J. Baskin*

When I was growing up in Sheboygan, Wisconsin, the days leading up to Rosh Hashanah yielded some of the most delectable smells and taste treats of the entire Jewish year.

Then when I was married and the mother of two, we didn't live anywhere near family, and if we were going to have the type of warm and inviting family celebrations I remembered, we were going to have to create it ourselves. I remember thinking that it would be "nice for the children," but it was just as much for me. We could bring them traditional food. Could we succeed?

My husband was a congregational rabbi, and from the time our children were small, I worked outside the home, and time was at a premium for both of us. We looked at it as a challenge, planned carefully, worked hard, and over time, created something special.

I began baking a month before, and the freezer was my new best friend. Once I had made my mother-in-law's special "worth-every-minute-of-it" challah, my grandma's holiday coffeecake, my mother's honey cake, and my Nana's poppy seed cookies, as well as other baked delights for desserts, everything else seemed to fall into place. Silver got polished, and linens were checked and pressed. I never seemed to serve fewer than 12 at a meal, so I always prepared in quantity.

I learned that the oven was happy to work even if I was not in the kitchen, so I roasted many a brisket or a turkey overnight, took it out in the morning, and chilled it during the work day. My husband sliced it at night, and everything was carefully labeled and stacked in the freezer or refrigerator, ready for heating in preparation for serving.

Homemade gefilte fish was always a favorite appetizer when we were growing up, and I was determined to provide the same for my own family. Lake Michigan-raised as I was, gefilte fish made from anything but whitefish and pike (with a little trout mixed in) was unthinkable. Landlocked as we were, getting whitefish and pike (forget the trout!) was not easy.

The solution came to me almost by accident. I was at the grocery store, in the frozen kosher section, and I saw frozen "bricks" of gefilte fish. I took one home, cooked it according to the package directions, and thought, "not bad." I looked at the wrapper and realized that the fish was made with whitefish and pike. What if I DON'T follow the directions? What if I defrost the frozen fish, mix it with matzo meal, lots of seasoning (a lot of white pepper! My rule of thumb is to be able to smell the pepper in the raw fish, then I know that I have enough, and cook it in stock with lots of seasoning (more white pepper, a little salt) lots of vegetables (celery, carrots and a lot of onion powder and onions). No matter, how bad can it be?

I dashed back to the same store, bought another fish brick, and did NOT follow the directions. It worked just as I thought, and have been making it in quantity for Rosh Hashanah ever since. With apologies to Mrs. Manischewitz and Mrs. Rokeach, no matter how it would taste, it is still better than the "fish from the jar."

Now both of our children are grown and have asked if the baked holiday delicacies they remembered could be theirs again. "It just wouldn't taste like Rosh Hashanah and Yom Kippur otherwise." So again last year, I began baking a month out, and the freezer was once again my best friend. The United Parcel Service was my second best friend, as the kids' packages arrived in time for Rosh Hashanah. Ours was on the table, just as it had been for so many years before. The special sweetness was mine, then it was ours, and now it is also theirs to savor, to share, and to recreate as they wish. Did we succeed? I think so.

—*Susie Drazen*

* * *

One month before Rosh Hashanah, I was in the hospital for breast cancer surgery. I remember my room being filled with dear friends. Since then, the High Holidays have meant wonderful family and friendship to me.

—*Marti Rosen-Atherton*

The harvest and preparation and sharing of food have encouraged gatherings of individuals since the beginning of time. And the common themes of fellowship and remembrance are universal and unrestricted by faith. Although I'm not Jewish, I believe all people are able to relate to the experience of sharing meals regardless of their religion.

—*Carol Evans Lynch*

* * *

My family had all the holiday meals at our house when I was a child. I was always the server and my sister was the dishwasher. At the end of the meal my uncles each left me a $1.00 tip by their plate. That's not bad when you have five uncles.

—*Judy Katskee*

The roto rooter man was a regular guest at our high holidays. My mom would begin cooking the day before and potato peels and eggshells would start filling up the sink. Invariably, the sink and disposal would get clogged around 6 p.m., and she'd be screaming till we called the roto rooter man to come fix it.

—*Pam Friedlander*

My childhood memories of the High Holidays are pleasure mixed with pain.

While all the non-Jewish kids got new outfits for Easter and Christmas, we got ours for Rosh Hashanah and Yom Kippur. And since our lunar-calendared holidays landed somewhere in the fall, the stores were freshly laden with fit-for-the-next-season dresses, skirts and sweaters spun from the sheerings of sheep.

So there I would be at synagogue, satiated with shopping and bedecked in my personally selected autumnal finery as the Orthodox Rabbi would lead us in prayer.

Did I mention that I lived in the Midwest where the September/October temperatures often rivaled those in July/August?

Did I mention that my Place of Worship was not air-conditioned?

Oh yes, and did I mention that I was allergic to wool?

Everybody else would be following along in their best Hebrew while I was silently, hopelessly, itchily begging

God in my best English NOT to write my name in the Book of Life next year since I planned to die of either hives or embarrassment within the next twenty-five minutes.

My mother spent more time telling me to stop squirming than she did renouncing her sins. As for MY sins—who cared? I was in agony and God was completely indifferent. I swore that when I grew up, I would NEVER go through High Holiday Hell again.

Well, I grew up years ago and have been true to my oath ever since. Each fall finds me in a fully air-conditioned temple, lotioned from head to toe and wearing fabrics a sheep wouldn't be caught dead in.

—*Rita Paskowitz*

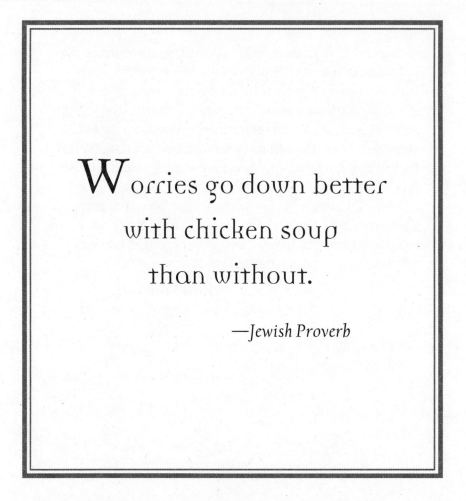

Worries go down better
with chicken soup
than without.

—*Jewish Proverb*

4

Home for the Holidays

Whether home is Israel, India, Atlanta, Montreal, or a mountaintop in Colorado.

Home for the holidays to me
is always Beth El synagogue.
I can look around the sanctuary and
imagine all of my relatives who used
to be sitting here too—especially my
mom, looking very snazzy in a new outfit.
Then there was my Aunt Betty,
a bit over dressed in one of those fox furs
with the eyes that glared back at me, and
the head and tails that wrapped around
her neck. And who could forget Aunt Rose
—everything's better in St. Louis—green?
—*Nancy Rips*

High Holidays are different in Israel. Yom Kippur is widely observed by most Jews in one way or another, even if only by refraining from doing anything at that time. But Rosh Hashanah is a great getaway time. When else do Israelis have two days off like that? So even if synagogues are full, the beaches, campsites and resorts are even fuller.

In Israel, the secular Jew identifies with Jewishness ethnically, nationalistically, sometimes culturally, but not religiously. Rosh Hashanah is of relatively little importance. Yom Kippur still seems to have at least a hold on most people's feelings. Perhaps it is guilt or simply identification with the one day when everything here shuts down.

—*Reuven Hammer*

* * *

Growing up in Montreal, I used to lay tefillin and attend morning services. But my worst Yom Kippur was when I was playing football. I had to go to synagogue instead of practice. The coach replaced me and I never got my position back.

—*William Shatner*

When I think of Rosh Hashanah, my first thought is not of the shofar or going to services or getting new clothes or missing school or attending family dinners. Instead, my mind transports me back to my childhood home, and back to a pretty park in the middle of the city.

Elmwood Park is today a large welcoming public space with sports fields, playground equipment, picnic tables, a golf course, and walking trails. When my parents were growing up, the park was considered out in the suburbs. Now it is midtown.

Each year on Rosh Hashanah afternoon, members of my home synagogue, the conservative shul in town, and members of the local orthodox synagogue would meet at a secluded stone patio overlooking a small stream in the park. Some who were more observant walked to the park, but most of us drove.

Most years I went with my dad. The drive was pleasant, and we would talk about the year just ending and the year upcoming. He always drove convertibles, and in my mind's eye, those drives for Tashlich were always a bit brisk, as fall was coming.

We'd gather together with the others and after saying a few prayers and singing a few melodies, we'd toss bread crumbs into the water. Those crumbs were symbols for our shortcomings, and we used the bread crumbs to physically toss aside our mistakes. But in choosing bread crumbs, an amazing thing happened. Our shortcomings became nourishment for the creatures in the water. Our mistakes, seemingly useless, became useful!

Tashlich became the most important moment of Rosh Hashanah for me, and it helped me see that I had the ability to act on the change we'd prayed about all day in the synagogue. Tashlich taught me that even my worst mistake could have some value. Tashlich taught me that while we repent and consider change on our own in prayer, we can join together in community to act on that change. Tashlich taught me that when we come together and actively pursue change, our world becomes more complete. Above all, Tashlich taught me that my life–including my worst moments—remains infused by holiness.

—*Rabbi Daniel Fellman*

Two things largely influence a Moroccan Rosh Hashanah menu: what one should eat and what one shouldn't eat. Dark foods, such as prunes and black olives, are considered taboo because they are thought to provide an ominous start to the year. In accordance with Jewish custom, Moroccans hope that sweet foods will set a good tone for the upcoming months, and so they serve even meat and vegetables—such as eggplant—with sugar.

Such pairings might seem unusual to the palates of American Jews accustomed to apples and honey, but these dishes are common throughout the region and are a much anticipated treat on Rosh Hashanah.

—*Aaron Kagan*

* * *

The most Jewish I ever felt was one Rosh Hashanah in India. I was living there, working as a correspondent for National Public Radio, and decided at the last minute to attend the New Year services at the one and only synagogue in New Delhi. It was a tiny box of a building and unbelievably hot inside. There was no air conditioning, only a couple of ceiling fans that stirred up the stale air. The congregation consisted of Indian Jews—women in beautiful saris—Israeli diplomats and a few stray expat Jews such as myself. The service was nothing spectacular but it was touching and comforting and I realized then what a minority we Jews are in the world. I'll never forget that.

—*Eric Weiner*

* * *

People call me the "Adventure Rabbi," because we hike, bike, and practice yoga every year during our Rosh Hashanah Retreat in Colorado. Like our Biblical ancestors, we return to the wilderness to welcome the New Year. Everyone leaves their fancy synagogue clothes behind and comes to pray together at 9,000 feet!

The outdoor service begins with songs and psalms, intended to help us "warm-up" before we pray. Then we walk together as a community, stopping often to slow ourselves down and be inspired by the majesty surrounding us.

The New Year is a time to evaluate the year that has passed, make amends, and set goals for the year ahead, and we offer people a myriad of outdoor activities to do this important work.

—Rabbi Jaime Korngold

* * *

One year I spent Rosh Hashanah in Kampula, Uganda. Everyone wore their best clothes and friends and relatives greeted each other. People prayed in the clearing under the clouds in front of the Kampula skyline. There was a man with one leg, five women, and 32 children. After the prayers, the young children ate ice cream in shades of bright pink and pastel orange. And at my friend's house, her sister visiting from Nairobi made a sweet called Tambi. She deep fried noodles, added sugar, vanilla, and cardamom, and then boiled the whole concoction. It made me think of kugel. And their sweet soda called Mirinda had the color, taste, and syrupy residue of Manishevitz.

—Scarlett Lionat

My family is originally from an area around Caracas, Venezuela. Most of my relatives live there, with some scattered in Central America and the Caribbean. Growing up, I learned Spanish first and eventually eased into English, but for a long time, I just assumed it was normal for one's family to be 10, 20 people strong, that eating platanos y caraotas con arroz (plantains with black beans and rice) was just as normal as eating a burger with fries, and that when your parents spoke to you in Spanish, you were in trouble.

Soon after my parents moved to the United States in 1981, my father started to reconnect with his Jewish roots from his mother's side, and I started to learn more about my religion. I started going to K'tantan (the kids service) at age four, went to Hebrew school, and learned about Jewish rituals and the life cycle. Every time I learned something new, I had such a wonderful experience and I learned from my growth, as best as an elementary school kid can. However, I never thought it could go hand in hand with my Latino roots. I didn't think it was really that possible. So, for many years I kept the two separate. Each side of me was very much a part of my existence, but never did they meld together to form one identity that I was comfortable with. I just didn't know how to be both at the same time.

It wasn't until I started my cantorial studies in Israel in the fall of 2007, that I realized this misconception was nowhere near true, and what was even better, I was able to learn how normal it was for Latinos to be Jews, and I opened myself to learn and grow.

Out of the blue one day, I was checking Facebook when my cantor back home, Gaston Bogomolni, and sent me a message saying: "Please let me know about your interest in doing something for the High Holidays, as I can have something really interesting for you." Well, after a few exchanges with the synagogue in the Dominican Republic, the congregation agreed to take on a woman cantor. It actually was a shocker for me when I heard those two words, "woman cantor." Would I be able to perform the way they are hoping?

I touched down on Caribbean soil for the first time that day, not really knowing what I was getting into but I couldn't wait to begin this journey.

After I got my bags from the baggage claim, I just couldn't shake off this feeling of "I am really here, and I'm really doing this"—a feeling that would accompany me until my flight home. A woman, Edith, was the first to greet me, and instead of a Dominican accent, a very familiar melody came from her lips, "Are you Annelise?"—the New York accent came ringing from the tops of her voice. A huge sigh of relief came over me.

Now granted, I am able to communicate in Spanish, but with all the excitement that came over me, I was better at expressing myself and asking questions in English. Edith and I talked about the community and its survival. In 1938, the Avien Conference in France was established, and 32 countries came together to realize the issue with Anti-Semitism rapidly creeping, and there was something that needed to be done to support the German and Austrian Jews. So, which country would grant them asylum? Of these 32 countries, including the United States, Australia, Germany, and Austria, the Dominican Republic was the only one who raised their hand to help. Although the ill-minded dictator Rafael Trujillo had ulterior motives to gentrify his country, his intentions nonetheless led to the saving of many souls that had not been acknowledged by so many during that time—and I immediately felt a bond with Edith (she is a second-generation citizen; born and raised in Sosua) and the history that brought me to Sosua. One by one I started to learn about the community—that they were ready to open their arms to me, but I still was not ready to run towards them.

As the days progressed towards Rosh Hashanah, I kept reviewing my nusach (melodies) and songs, but then it hit me. I needed to stop thinking about the logistics and focus on the real task at hand—communicating with God. How was I going to feel to be the voice, the soul, the anguish and solemn feelings of the day and in the shaping of a brand New Year for the many I would represent? But more importantly, how would I take all my worries and love of God and relay that in my davening, my praying? So, with all these feelings, and from what my cantor had told me about the community, I took their enthusiasm to feel a connection to the service, their openness to try a new way and took my time and freed my spirit and sung to God to usher in the New Year.

As each person poured into the ever-so-tiny sanctuary that held at most 60 people, I became more hopeful as each seat was filling up. Hollers of "Hola, como estas?" followed by warm hugs and kisses, talks about parents, family, and how business was going filled the sanctuary. I realized among the faces of newly immigrated Israelis, native born first-, second-, and third-generation Sosuans and visitors who'd been coming several times to even first timers, all had that look when they first took sight of me—am I ready? And I replied smiling, "Let's do this together." The rest is history. We had a great community dinner afterwards, and immediately I had been inducted into their community as their adopted daughter.

Thanks to the simple Jewish community of Sosua, I rediscovered myself, and it changed my life forever.

—*Annelise Ocanto*

The most breathtaking High Holiday experience for me was being at the Western Wall in the Old City of Jerusalem during Rosh Hashanah and Yom Kippur.

We saw a young man wearing a black hat and suit. He was frantically waving his arms to a swarm of people approaching him. My husband was intrigued and went to meet him. He came back to tell me this person was from the Student Information Center, and he matched people who wanted a place to go for the holidays with another group who wanted guests for these special days.

He arranged for us to have a festive meal with a lovely young couple who lived in the heart of the old city. And on the second day, we were invited to a family's home who lived in Yemin Moshe, an area adjacent to the Old City.

That was the first year we left our family for the High Holidays. As a result, we made everlasting friendships, and now we are blessed with an even larger family.

—*Ruth Goldenberg*

One of the unique aspects of life in New Mexico is the inclusion of New Mexican chilies into the cuisine, even on Rosh Hashanah. The official state question is "Red or Green?" which refers to the choice of chilies.

—*Rabbi Art Flicker*

My family and I lived in Cincinnati for a number of years. One Yom Kippur, the Rabbi told the congregation that we needed to evacuate the synagogue immediately. We were concerned and filed out to the parking lot and lawn. The fire department was called because a gas leak was suspected. After a safety check, though, it was determined there was no immediate danger, but in order to ensure everyone's safety, the decision was made to hold services outside.

There was a small outdoor sanctuary, but most of us gathered on the lawn. The Torahs were brought outdoors, and we continued the service where we left off. It was a beautiful fall day, and I'll always remember saying the traditional prayers while watching the trees showing off their autumn finery. Observing those High Holidays in God's natural setting was spiritual and uplifting for my family. It will always be my favorite Yom Kippur.

—*Denise Ipock*

My husband and I were in the military for years. We became more religious overseas, because when you're away from family, you miss it even more. In Greece we observed the High Holidays in the middle of the week, because the traveling circuit Rabbi could only get there then. And I vividly recall being in Seoul, Korea, for Rosh Hashanah, where we prepared an all kosher dinner at their Retreat center.

—*Jane Dreyfus*

Rosh Hashanah is one of the most important Jewish holidays of the year, and we welcome New Zealand's Jewish community into Parliament to commemorate it. We have a small but vibrant Jewish population. The first synagogue was consecrated in Wellington in 1868. Today almost 7,000 people identify as Jewish, and our government recognizes that New Zealand is a place of diverse cultures and religions, and believes all New Zealanders are stronger for this diversity.

In past years, we've brought many different cultural and faith celebrations into Parliament, including the Muslim festival of Eid, the Hindu festival of Diwali, and the Chinese New Year.

Jewish immigrants have brought a passion for education, a devotion to family and community, and a strong social conscience to New Zealand. Our celebration of Rosh Hashanah recognizes this legacy, as well as the many contributions Jews continue to make to New Zealand. We hope this celebration will start a tradition of celebrating many Jewish festivals in Parliament.

—Ethnic Affairs Minister, Chris Carter

5

fast foods

*How do you stop thinking about food
when you aren't supposed to eat or drink
for an entire 25-hour period?*

Some people break the fast
with orange juice, maybe a bagel,
or a piece of bundt cake, but i break
the fast with a snickers candy bar.
Every year on Yom Kippur Day,
i fill my glove compartment in the
morning with snickers bars. The minute
the final shofar blast is sounded,
my kids and nephews and nieces
all know to meet outside in the parking
lot by my car for our non-official

break the fast treat.

—*Nancy Rips*

I always fast on Yom Kippur. When I was twelve, my mother got breast cancer and almost died from being over-radiated. I made a deal. I would fast if she could live. The operation was right before Rosh Hashanah, but the day before Yom Kippur, she got terribly sick again. It was horrible. She actually got a bone infection. But she survived, for twenty more years. That's when I started fasting and I've done it every year since then.

—*Tony Kushner*

* * *

Our family's Break-the-Fast dinner combines a ritual meal with a ritual debate about which is the better kugel —with raisins or without!

—*Ellen Frankel*

My mother's Yom Kippur Break-the-Fast was the highlight of the High Holiday season when I was young. There was cinnamon sweet kugel (always with raisins), fluffy, luscious, to die for herring in sour cream (with apples and lemon slices to look beautiful and little cocktail rye breads), lox and cream cheese (with red onions and tomatoes), bagels, and buttery, melt-in-your-mouth coffeecake (with streusel topping). Each bite of food was so unbelievably wonderful after a whole day of fasting. Of course, we always ate until we burst. But, oh, how delicious! Our entire family was there—cousins, aunts, uncles—except my beloved Uncle Leo, who always came late. I never understood it. He was so kind and would never be rude to anybody. So why was it that year after year, we were all feasting at 6 p.m. and he came at 7:45?

I was raised at a Reform temple, and I loved going to services, especially on Yom Kippur. The atmosphere in the sanctuary was always solemn and austere, but particularly so on Yom Kippur. The rabbi and cantor in their flowing white robes high up on the pulpit looked so very Biblical

—awesome and holy. In high school, I started attending the Neilah service, always at 5 p.m. As the sunlight streaming in through the magnificent stained glass windows began to dim toward the end of the service, I felt so peaceful, hopeful and hungry! I rushed home to my parents and other relatives and our delectable Break-the-Fast, where everyone enjoyed the most scrumptious feast you could imagine—except my Uncle Leo who appeared just before 8 p.m. My mother always made a plate for him and saved it, choosing all of his favorite foods in abundance, in case the rest of us ate everything before he got to the house.

After I got married, my husband, Dennis, and I became more observant and we learned the secret of Uncle Leo's late arrival. My mother always said of it, "They're so religious at the Conservative synagogue, their services go on forever," but now I knew why. Sundown on Yom Kippur wasn't at 6 p.m. It was at sundown—much later than our Temple. Uncle Leo wasn't late. He was right on time!

—*Susan Paley*

I have more fond memories about Yom Kippur than Rosh Hashanah. For a start, a game of the World Series always seemed to be taking place on Yom Kippur, and my father, being an avid baseball fan and not such an avid Jew, would dutifully go with my grandfather (his father-in-law) and me to synagogue in the morning, but would somehow disappear in early afternoon. We belonged to a Conservative, verging on Orthodox shul, and the services would last all day. He'd then walk home, draw all the blinds and shades on the windows, so no neighbors could possibly see what he was up to, and watch the game while eating Ritz crackers spread heavily with peanut butter. Everyone in our neighborhood went to shul on Yom Kippur so it was quite the social occasion. I remember all the women in mink stoles, even though it might be 90 degrees and everyone wearing their new, New Year finery. Standing outside synagogue was even more important than going in. Everyone saw you outside. During Yiskor, it was a mob scene outside because, of course, only mourners were inside.

We broke the fast with a dairy spread. We always thought it was weird that our neighbors, the Meyers, started with oatmeal, as if it was really breakfast. We started with pickled herring, then moved on to a huge spread of smoked fish and salads—tuna, egg salad, and years later we added whitefish salad—various cheeses, plus bagels, sour rye (cornbread in NYC), pumpernickel and onion buns. After that dairy spread, we had the major indulgence of the meal, my grandmother's noodle kugel, the recipe for which is in my book, *Jewish Home Cooking: Yiddish Recipes Revisited*. It wasn't sweet, so we had many cakes and pastries after that.

—*Arthur Schwartz*

* * *

Yom Kippur is like instant Lent.

—*Leo Rosten*

So there it was, early afternoon on Yom Kippur Day. The scene: the old Litvisher shul on 19th and Burt Streets. The cast of characters: four teenage girls, with not a single driver's license between them.

As boredom set in, somebody suggested somehow getting the keys to her dad's car and slipping out for a little ride. Who would know? All the parents were in shul, fasting and davening. The bravest managed to get the keys and we piled into the car. I don't know where we were going, but three blocks away from the starting point, as we went through the intersection, we were hit broadside by a WPA truck. Guess who was sitting right in the exact place that was hit?

I woke up in the emergency room of the hospital, unable to say anything except "My dad is gonna kill me!"

Fortunately, he didn't, but I took a lot of abuse from people telling me that's what we got for skipping out of shul, riding on Yom Kippur, and swiping a car.

My poor mom walked around for days, just shaking her head. Nobody believed the chutzpah it took. When I think back to that long ago afternoon, neither can I. It happened some 70 years ago! And I'll tell you another secret: I've never gotten into a car on Yom Kippur without remembering the Yom Tov we swiped the car to go for a ride!

—*Bert Lewis*

* * *

I remember the first time I ate on Yom Kippur, and I thought, "You know if I'm wrong, then there probably is a death sentence." So I took the Woody Allen approach of "I don't believe in an afterlife, but I'm taking a change of underwear just in case."

—*Jason Alexander*

* * *

I really like eating, but the hunger associated with fasting is really helpful. You think about how you've wronged your friends and how you should change in the future.

—*Natalie Portman*

I loved my mother's honey cakes! After I got married and moved away, my mother always baked one before Rosh Hashanah and mailed it to me. Even though she never used a recipe, the cakes often sank in the middle and were often a little hard to chew; I enjoyed the taste and especially the love that went into them. We always broke the fast on the way home from synagogue with her honey cake and grapes.

—*Gilda Pieck*

* * *

O n Rosh Hashanah you pig out and Yom Kippur you fast.

—*Stephanie Lerner*

* * *

I always fasted on Yom Kippur because it scared me not to. This holiday is about who should live, who should die. Even when I worked on Yom Kippur, which I wouldn't do now, I fasted. Of course, my focus wasn't on food—you try making love to Lana Turner on an empty stomach.

—*Kirk Douglas*

Break the fast is our busiest time of the year at Zabars. Four men start making bagels at 3:30 a.m., and the staff expects to sell more than 600 dozen in one day. It's like the Jewish Olympics in here.

—David Tait

* * *

We observe Rosh Hashanah and Yom Kippur. Nobody's compelled to fast, but I fast and Kate does, too.

—Steven Spielberg

* * *

I generally fasted as a teenager, inevitably getting a headache from it. One year, however, I went to a friend's home during the afternoon break and there, horrible of horribles, I had a small sip of 7-Up. Not a whole bottle, mind you. This resulted in great pangs of guilt, but obviously the memory has lingered.

—Howard Kaslow

Pastrami killed more Jews than
the Holocaust. so you better believe
Jews mean business on Yom Kippur.
it's the perfect penance for
a food-oriented culture.
Not only are you forced to
confront the past year's worth of
transgressions, you have to do it
on an empty stomach.

—*Jerry Lewis*

6

Repentance Means Having to Say You're Sorry

A serious chapter based on the words of Elie Weisel:
"The one sin God cannot forgive
is against our fellowman.
Only humans have the right to forgive each other."

The ten-day period between Rosh Hashanah & Yom Kippur are known as the Days of Awe. It's a period when you are supposed to reflect on the past year & try to make amends with the people you may have harmed. It's my busiest week of the year!

—*Nancy Rips*

We abuse, we betray, we are cruel.
We destroy, we embitter, we falsify.
We gossip, we hate, we insult.
We jeer, we kill, we lie.
We mock, we neglect, we oppress.
We pervert, we quarrel, we rebel.
We steal, we transgress, we are unkind.
We are violent, we are wicked, we are xenophobic.
We yield to evil, we are zealots for bad causes.

For all of these, O god of forgiveness,
forgive us, pardon us, grant us atonement.

—*A Yom Kippur Prayer*

What never ceases to impress me about these prayers is their focus on "we" and "us," rather than "I" and "me." What Yom Kippur defines as sins—even crimes like robbery, violence, and licentiousness—are seen as the responsibility of the entire community. For this reason, rather than just confessing individually and in solitude, we confess together and in public. However much individuals are responsible for their own transgressions, the rest of us, the prayer suggests, are not wholly blameless.

—*Jonathan Sarna*

* * *

On Yom Kippur, my mother used to call relatives with whom she had been bickering. Each year when I was little, I overheard her apologizing to people she didn't like. She explained, "On Yom Kippur, not liking was irrelevant and arguing was not an option."

Then one year recently, I got a card from my ex-husband, apologizing for his part in our miserable marriage.

The card came 30 years after the fact. I was astonished. A feeling of relief washed over me. I guess I had thought everything wrong in the marriage was my fault.

—*Dr. Marilyn Kallet*

* * *

If a person hurt you so terribly, he doesn't deserve the right to loom so large in your mind. He doesn't deserve the power to make you a bitter, resentful person, to change your personality for the worse. You want to get even with him? You don't get even by continuing to hurt, by continuing to seethe with rage so that you can't enjoy the life you have. You get even by letting go, so that he can no longer pull your emotional strings.

—*Harold Kushner*

My favorite holiday
is Yom Kippur.
I believe
in second chances.

—*Rabbi Margaret Moers Wenig*

At times it is easy to forgive. Other times it is very difficult.

At times we have to forgive. Other times we must not forgive.

We must not forgive a grandpa who murdered his granddaughter.

We must not forgive a mother who drowned her child.

We must not forgive someone who murdered his friend at a club.

We must not forgive someone who got behind the wheel intoxicated and high and murdered six people.

We must not forgive the man who murdered his wife.

We must not forgive the man who raped his daughter.

We must not forgive people who tortured the elderly.

We must not forgive the woman who poured acid on a soldier and blinded him.

We must not forgive the man who went on a bulldozer rampage and murdered civilians, including a pregnant mother.

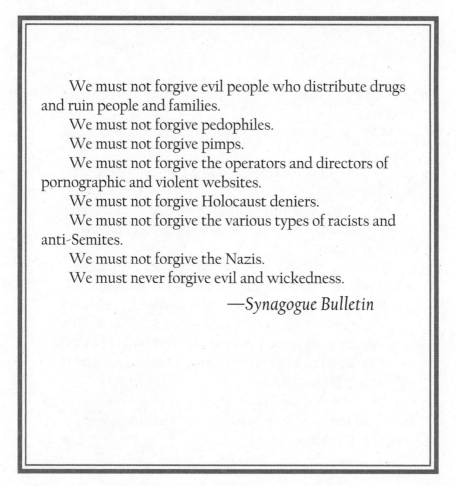

We must not forgive evil people who distribute drugs and ruin people and families.

We must not forgive pedophiles.

We must not forgive pimps.

We must not forgive the operators and directors of pornographic and violent websites.

We must not forgive Holocaust deniers.

We must not forgive the various types of racists and anti-Semites.

We must not forgive the Nazis.

We must never forgive evil and wickedness.

—*Synagogue Bulletin*

We have a new project in Washington, D.C. inspired by the popular books and website "PostSecret." People send anonymous secrets to liberate themselves and comfort others. These are personal reflections for a project called "Post Regret," and they are hung anonymously around the walls of the Temple. Many spoke of how they had treated friends or family, while some addressed ways in which people hurt themselves by lacking discipline or holding in emotions.

—*Annie Atherton*

* * *

Rosh Hashanah teaches that we live in a world in which humans bear responsibility for their actions. They have the opportunity to look into themselves, take stock of their behavior, and change what they know to be wrong.

—*Francine Klagsbrun*

The tenth day of the seventh month shall be your day of atonement, a day to search your soul, a sacred day.

—*Leviticus 23:27*

* * *

Yom Kippur is a day to ponder one's mistakes of the previous year and consider resolutions for the next. I think one of the keys to my happiness is that I try to catch my mistakes and transgressions as quickly as possible after the fact and minimize the period of reflection.

—*Michael J. Fox*

* * *

In the Jewish tradition there are two kinds of forgiveness: one kind is what God can give and the other is what man can give. There are things that men do to each other where God does not intervene. For instance, on the eve of Yom

Kippur, the Day of Atonement, the most important day in our year, we ask God to forgive us. We ask him to forgive us for all kinds of sins committed. But one sin he cannot forgive is the sin I commit against a fellow human being. Only that human being has the right to forgive me. And, that right has its limitations. If I ask that person to forgive me three times and that person says no, then the blame is on him or her. Then they have to offer forgiveness for not forgiving.

—*Elie Wiesel*

* * *

Never mind the remorse, just don't do what causes it.

—*Jewish Saying*

True repentance is a continuous year-round process, but it's still good to have a failsafe built into the system. A Jew hasn't been that succinct since Moses hit us with the *Ten Commandments*. The point is that I love Yom Kippur. It's the one day of the year where the Jewish community can come together to feel guilty and suffer. Most of us do it every day—it's just nice to have the company.

—*Josh Howie*

* * *

"For example" is not proof.

—*Yiddish Folk Saying*

Watch your thoughts; they become your words. Watch your words; they become your actions. Watch your actions; they become your habits. Watch your habits; they become your character. Watch your character, for it will become your destiny.

—*Rabbi Hillel*

* * *

Yom Kippur fashion is hard, but one solution I observed was the custom on Erev Yom Kippur for people to dress in light colors: beige, off-white, banana. It was a wonderful thing, all those people throwing away their sins in shades of white. I think it's considered disrespectful on this holiday to wear leather or animal skin, which is another reason to get your fur-trimmed thrills at Rosh Hashanah. On Yom Kippur everyone is supposed to jump on the Stella McCartney bandwagon and wear synthetic shoes. What about a divine pair of satin Prada platform clogs? Or velvet clogs from Marc Jacobs with socks? That's a sin anyone could atone for.

—*Isaac Mizrahi*

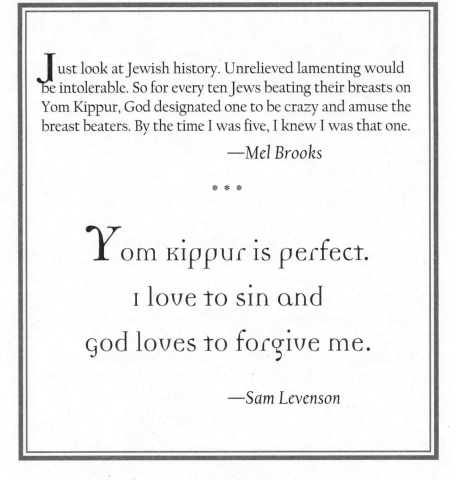

Just look at Jewish history. Unrelieved lamenting would be intolerable. So for every ten Jews beating their breasts on Yom Kippur, God designated one to be crazy and amuse the breast beaters. By the time I was five, I knew I was that one.

—*Mel Brooks*

* * *

Yom kippur is perfect.
I love to sin and
god loves to forgive me.

—*Sam Levenson*

Two old friends who have been arguing the entire year decided they should meet before Yom Kippur and try to make up. Brian says, "I forgive you for any wrongs you did to me. And I ask that you forgive me, too." Alan responds, "I forgive you, and I wish for you in the coming year all that you wish for me."

"Oh, man," Brian replies, "You're starting again already?"

—*Synagogue Bulletin*

If you want the present
to be different from the past,
study the past.

—*Baruch Spinoza*

* * *

No man suffers
for another's sins.
He has enough of his own.

—*Alan King*

7

who wrote
the Book of Life?

*We all try to be included in the Book of Life,
which is written on Rosh Hashanah
and sealed on Yom Kippur.*

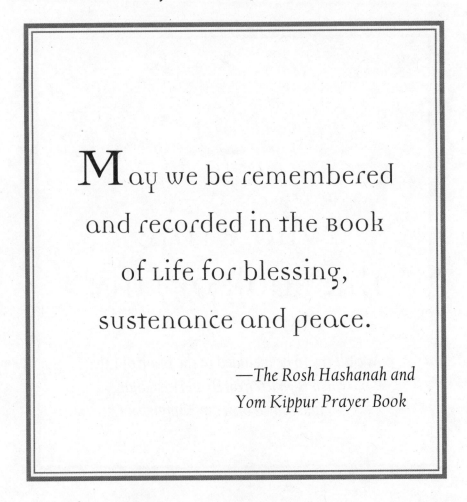

May we be remembered
and recorded in the book
of life for blessing,
sustenance and peace.

—*The Rosh Hashanah and
Yom Kippur Prayer Book*

When I think about the Book of Life, I first think about who has died in the past few year. Then I can't help but think about who might be dying in the next few years. It's overwhelming to realize we have such little control over our own lives, that we are such small, probably insignificant, parts of the entire universe. But that doesn't mean we can stop trying to be significant.

—*Nancy Rips*

* * *

Do all the good you can,
By all the means you can,
In all the ways you can,
In all the places you can,
At all the times you can,
To all the people you can,
As long as ever you can.

—*John Wesley*

Every year as we begin Rosh Hashanah and Yom Kippur, we reflect on our stories and take a deep look at the story of our lives and our journeys. The High Holidays come to help us shape our story and rebalance our moral compasses. Our stories are both particular and universal at the same time. We each have unique parts of our own story while there are common themes that are shared by many of us.

Rosh Hashanah and Yom Kippur are two aspects of our story. Rosh Hashanah begins with the universal and through the Ten Days of Repentance and Yom Kippur we weave our tale from universal to particular to the universal impact of our individual story. For the message of these days is that we matter. Our lives matter. Our actions and our words matter. And that we can in the end have an impact on our world and our lives. Hopefully over the course of these High Holidays your stories will be shared and written and rewritten with deeper meaning, greater clarity of purpose and, God willing, many additional chapters!

—*Rabbi Denise L. Eger*

Lest we think that God sealing our name and fate into the Book of Life on Yom Kippur is a mere metaphor, consider the fate of my grandfather, the late Harry Hahn. In the 1930s, he was a healthy man in his 50s. Then on one unusually cold, rainy Yom Kippur day, he contracted pneumonia walking home from the synagogue. By Sukkot, four days later, he was dead. If that does not exemplify swift judgment, I don't know what does.

—*Aveva Skukert*

* * *

It took a priest to make me a Jew. I knew I was Jewish, but I knew very little about Judaism. I went to Hebrew School and learned to read Hebrew by rote and without meaning. I went to Sunday school. I never got past the Bible Stories in Genesis, nor did I ever see them as anything but stories. I knew about the Jewish holidays, mostly about the foods associated with the holiday and enjoyed sharing holiday meals with extended family.

My family observed the High Holidays with special foods. We went to the synagogue, visited with congregants, opened the prayer book, but did very little praying. My fondest memories of Rosh Hashanah were of my mother's brisket.

So there I was, a 16-year-old Jewish illiterate attending Creighton University, matching wits with the engaging, knowledgeable Jesuit priest, who was excited about his Catholicism. I was intrigued by his knowledge and his enthusiasm about his religion. My mother's brisket couldn't hold a candle to his description of the virgin birth of Jesus. I gave my parents some sleepless nights with my questions about Judaism they couldn't answer. My interest in Catholicism grew and I was on the brink of thoughts about conversion. I asked many questions about Catholic beliefs and my Jesuit friend had reasonable answers until we hit a snag.

We had several sessions discussing the "Holy Trinity." I had a hard time with the concept of "The Father, the Son, and the Holy Spirit." The answers to my questions about the Trinity clashed with my pragmatism. In frustration I remember the priest saying, "My child, you have to have faith and believe in the Trinity and the Virgin birth." And I remember saying, "Not if I stay Jewish I don't." It was a major turning point in my life that led me to finding out what "staying Jewish" really meant.

That was the end of my discussions with the priest and the beginning of my search for what it meant to be Jewish. I read books about Jewish philosophy, Jewish history, Jewish ethics, and Jewish prayer. I talked to rabbis and other Jewish scholars. I learned the true meaning of the holidays, and it all made such sense. Judaism made no demands on my beliefs. The emphasis was on what I did —not what I believed. It was "grown up" Judaism, and I loved what I was learning. My parents had no more sleepless nights. The priest and I remained friends, although we never discussed religion again.

The following September, the High Holidays were exciting for me. For the first time, I spent more time in the synagogue praying than visiting with friends on the steps of the synagogue. I understood the purpose and the promise of the Jewish New Year, the Yom Kippur prayers had real meaning. I understood the meaning of repentance, I talked directly to God and had no need for the "Son or the Holy Spirit" to intervene for me. In the lingo of today, I guess you could say I was "a reborn Jew."

The High Holidays that year took me into the world of adult Judaism. I still have fond memories of my mother's brisket and holiday dinners with family. I also have thankful memories of the Catholic priest who played a key role in leading me to a meaningful Jewish life.

—*Mickey Greenberg*

* * *

There are so many great things about Judaism, especially the fact that we have Yom Kippur where you spend the whole day in atonement, thinking about your mistakes and taking responsibility for them.

—*Kyra Sedgwick*

I had no religious education. I'm Jewish because my parents are, but my father considered himself an atheist and religion was not a part of my family's life. I never went to Sunday school or Temple, and I never observed Yom Kippur. However, on that day, I never went on the air, and I still don't.

—*Barbara Walters*

* * *

Don't wait for
the last judgment.
It takes place every day.

—*Albert Camus*

One morning while we were on vacation in Milwaukee, Ariella, our three-year-old, had requested that her Grandpa Sherm make pancakes with her. She showed him where the Bisquick was and I could hear her from our room, as I dragged myself from sleep, instructing him what needed to be done, and in what order, to properly cook up the perfect pancakes. As the pancakes came off the griddle, Grandpa Sherm placed a plate of warm, delicious hotcakes in front of his granddaughter. I sauntered into the kitchen at that moment. Ariella took one look at the plate and then broke down in hysterics. Sobbing uncontrollably, as only a three-year-old can, she managed to explain that "You're supposed to cut the pancakes first *then* put the syrup on." Somehow, Grandpa Sherm had neglected this important consideration by prematurely pouring the syrup.

We had made pancakes countless times before, yet I had never really paid much attention to the precise steps we had gone through to make our pancakes. Obviously, Ariella had. For her, each activity and its order along the way had become part of a sacred ritual!

It dawned on me that so much of our life is beyond our control (no matter how much we may protest to the contrary). And so many times we are left trying to make sense of what has happened to us. Our years comprise a lifetime of rituals, of the holy and the mundane, bringing order, stability, security, and, yes, a sense of control into our world. Like a stack of pancakes, each of our lives is prepared just so, everything in its place. For the most part, we're able to keep things together, carefully orchestrating and structuring as we go; we organize ourselves at a dizzying pace. Remove one thing and change one component, though, and we are strangely unsettled, left unbalance.

My daughter's experience with the pancakes reminds me why these are, in fact, the Days of Awe, in the truest sense of the work. During those ten days between Rosh Hashanah and Yom Kippur, we come face-to face with the uncontrollable, the unknowable. The ultimate cause for existential panic! In life, we may not get our pancakes the way we like them or are used to them. Experiencing days of fear and trembling, we are rightfully filled with anxiety as we contemplate the year ahead. "Who shall live and who shall die?" These are questions from the High Holiday liturgy to which we, who are used to having all the answers, have no answer or control over the outcome. The Days of Awe remind us that we don't have any guarantees about the future, and that we must live fully and nobly in the shadow of great uncertainty. When we were young we had regular exposure to our powerlessness, we understood we didn't make all the rules, we still knew how to cry in the face of such awesome vulnerability.

As adults, we have convinced ourselves that we are in control, and that we are invincible, that we don't need to cry. The essence of the High Holidays is reintroducing us to our vulnerability, allowing us to confront our weaknesses and frailties, challenging us to recognize our need for others and for God in our lives. Only then may we begin to live with a sense of humility and appreciation for the precious gift of life that is ours.

—*Rabbi Greg Wolfe*

My friends and I prepare 75 to 100 care packages filled with honey sticks, dried apples, gefilte fish, chap stick, deodorant, and other nonperishable items. The boxes are shipped to platoons in Iraq, Kuwait, and South Korea to be distributed among Jewish soldiers just in time for Rosh Hashanah. This is my way of giving back and helping Jewish soldiers.

—*Talia Shabes*

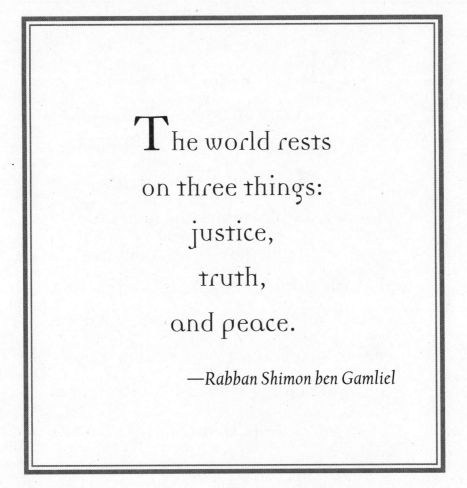

The world rests
on three things:
justice,
truth,
and peace.

—*Rabban Shimon ben Gamliel*

Every day
I read the obituary column,
and I don't get it
—people always die
in alphabetical order.

—James "Jimbo" Jagusch

People are dying who
have never died before.

—*Dr. Leon Fellman*

8

Let My People Enjoy

*Humor in Judaism dates back to Torah.
According to tradition, we are commanded
to sing, study, and enjoy the Jewish holidays.*

Every year my mother took me shopping for a new Rosh Hashanah outfit. we went to the fourth floor girls section of the old downtown Brandeis Department store. In the corner of the clothing area was on officious looking woman wearing a white nurse's uniform with matching white hat, white shoes, and a tape measure swung around her neck. she sold training bras. I always wondered what exactly they were training.

—*Nancy Rips*

Before the High Holidays, David needed to have his tallit cleaned. He called his friend to ask what dry cleaner to take it to. "I always take my tallit to the dry cleaner on West 34th St. He charges $24."

So David went and found that the ownership had changed. He asked the new owner, Mr. Walton, if he met the old prices. Mr. Walton assured him that he did.

Three days later, David goes to get his tallit and is given a bill for $240. He storms at Mr. Walton, "I thought you matched the old prices?"

"I did," said Mr. Walton, "$24 for the tallit, but it was $240 to get all the knots out of the fringes."

—*Synagogue Bulletin*

synagogue seating Request form for Yom Kippur

During the last holiday season, many individuals expressed concern over the seating arrangements in the synagogue. In order for us to place you in a seat which will best suit you, we ask you to complete the following questionnaire and return it to the synagogue office as soon as possible.

1. I would prefer to sit in the ... (check one)
____Talking section
____No talking section

2. If talking, which category do you prefer?
(Indicate order of interest.)
____Stock market
____Sports
____Medicine
____General gossip

____Specific gossip (choose)
   __The rabbi
   __The cantor
   __The cantor's voice
   __The cantor's significant other
____Fashion news
____What others are wearing
____Why they look awful
____Your neighbors
____Your relatives
____Your neighbors' relatives
____Presidential Election (uh oh)
____Sex (Preference: _____)
____Who's cheating on/having an affair with whom
Other: _____

3. Which of the following would you like to be near for free professional advice?
____Doctor
____Dentist
____Nutritionist

____Psychiatrist
____Child psychiatrist
____Podiatrist
____Chiropractor
____Stockbroker
____Accountant
____Lawyer
____Criminal
____Civil
____Real estate agent
____ Architect
____Plumber
____Buyer (Specify store: _____)
____Sexologist
____Golf pro [tentative; we're still trying to find
     a Jewish one]
Other: _____

4. I want a seat located (indicate order of priority):
____On the aisle
____Near the exit

_____Near the window
_____In Aruba
_____Near the bathroom
_____Near my in-laws
_____As far away from my in-laws as possible
_____As far away from my ex-in-laws as possible
_____Near the pulpit
_____Near the Kiddush table
_____Near single men
_____Near available women
_____Where no one on the bimah can see/hear me
talking during services
_____Where no one will notice me sleeping during services
_____Where I can sleep during the rabbi's sermon
[additional charge]

5. Please do not place me anywhere near the following people: _____

—*The Jewish Magazine*

When Fred's wife died after a long illness, he decided he would get a new lease on life. He lost weight, went to a spa, and had plastic surgery. As he was leaving his house in his new designer suit, he was hit by a car and immediately died.

When he got to heaven, he asked his maker, "God, why me, now? I did everything. I was a good husband, always went to High Holiday services, and gave to charity. Why now, when I have a chance to live a little, did this happen to me?"

God replied, "To tell you the truth, Fred, I just didn't recognize you!"

—Apocryphal tale from a
Synagogue Bulletin

At my temple last year the Rabbi's sermon started off beautifully, examining Rosh Hashanah as the birthday of the world. But it quickly turned into a "go green" lecture: global warming, wasteful consumption, the need to conserve energy, etc. As the sermon went on and on, I turned to my daughter and suggested that, in order to actually conserve some energy, we find the light switches for the temple and turn them off. Her response: "And the mic, too."

—*Sam Kazman*

* * *

Dear God,
I love and respect you, so I'm not about to get cute. Besides at age 82 that could be shaky. But is there any chance of getting me better seats in Temple for the High Holidays?

—*Don Rickles*

It was the '50s, and on the High Holidays, we sat in the back of the synagogue with Mom's friends. That's where they had their little chat-fests. I don't know how old I was when I found out there was something going on up in the front!

— *Marilyn Robinson*

* * *

This year my granddaughter told me, "On Rosh Hashanah we have apples and honey for a sweet New Year."

"That's right," I said. "What else?"

"We eat a round challah with raisins."

"That sounds good," I told her. "Anything else special about the holiday?"

"Yes," she told me, "we get gift cards."

—*Estelle Silverman*

A synagogue has a problem. A family of squirrels is living in the building, and the Board of Directors vote to have the squirrels caught and released to a local forest preserve. They do it four times. And each time the squirrels come back to the synagogue.

Finally, the Board votes the squirrels in as members of the synagogue. It works just as they thought it might. Now the squirrels only turn up on Rosh Hashanah and Yom Kippur.

—*Synagogue Bulletin*

* * *

God is love, but get it in writing.

—*Gypsy Rose Lee*

I usually observe the major Jewish holidays, particularly Rosh Hashanah, so I can apologize for all the other ones I missed.

—*Ben Feldman*

* * *

My grandson Aaron, goes to a Jewish day school and knows about synagogue services. One year, when he was about 7, he was sitting next me on Yom Kippur. He saw a plaque on the wall that had names of people who were killed during the war. He asked what that meant.

I told him, "Those were people who died in the service." Aaron asked, "Morning or evening?"

—*Jake Mitchell*

* * *

I talk to myself during services because I like dealing with a better class of people.

—*Jackie Mason*

The first Jewish President of the United States has been inaugurated, and when it was almost time for Rosh Hashanah, he calls up his mother to invite her to the White House. Their conversation goes something like this:

Prez: Mom, with Rosh Hashanah coming up soon, I want you to celebrate it with us at the White House.

Mom: Oh, I don't know. I'll have to get to the airport and...

Prez: Mom! I'm the President of the United States! I'll send a limo for you. It will take you right to the airport!

Mom: OK, but when I get to the airport, I'll have to stand on the line to buy a ticket and check my baggage. Oh, it will be so difficult for me.

Prez: Mom, don't worry about standing on lines or any of that. I'm the most powerful person in the world. I'm the President. I'll send Air Force One for you!

Mom: Well, Ok. But when I get to Washington, I'll have to find a cab and. . . .

Prez: Mom, please! I'll have a helicopter waiting for you. It will bring you right to the White House lawn!

Mom: Well, yeah. But where will I stay? Can I get a hotel mom?

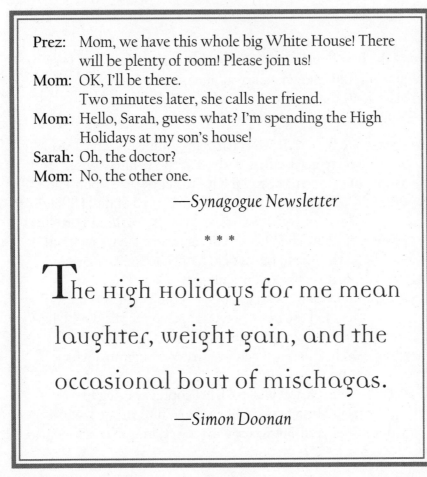

Prez: Mom, we have this whole big White House! There will be plenty of room! Please join us!

Mom: OK, I'll be there.

Two minutes later, she calls her friend.

Mom: Hello, Sarah, guess what? I'm spending the High Holidays at my son's house!

Sarah: Oh, the doctor?

Mom: No, the other one.

—*Synagogue Newsletter*

* * *

The High Holidays for me mean laughter, weight gain, and the occasional bout of mischagas.

—*Simon Doonan*

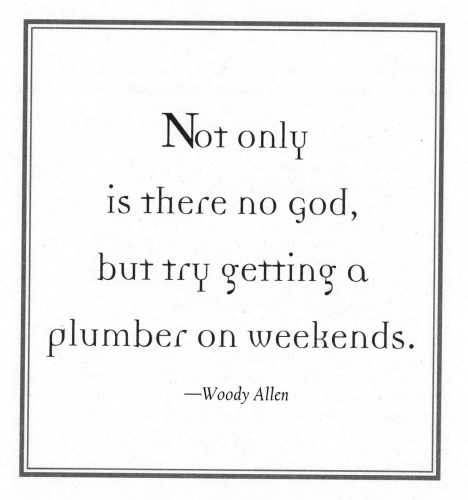

Not only
is there no god,
but try getting a
plumber on weekends.

—*Woody Allen*

May this Yom Tov find you seated around the dinner table together with your beloved family and cherished friends, ushering in the New Year ahead.

May you get a clean bill of health from your dentist, your cardiologist, your gastroenterologist, your urologist, your proctologist, your podiatrist, your psychiatrist, your gynecologist, your plumber, and the IRS.

May your hair, your teeth, your facelift, your abs, and your stocks not fall; and may your blood pressure, your triglycerides, your cholesterol, your white blood count, and your mortgage interest not rise.

May you remember to say "I love you" at least once a day to your spouse, your child, your parents, your friends; but not to your secretary, your nurse, your masseuse, your hairdresser, or your tennis instructor.

May we live as God intended, in a world at peace and the awareness of His love in every sunset, every flower's unfolding petals, every baby's smile, every lover's kiss, and every wonderful, astonishing, miraculous beat of our heart.

—Synagogue Bulletin

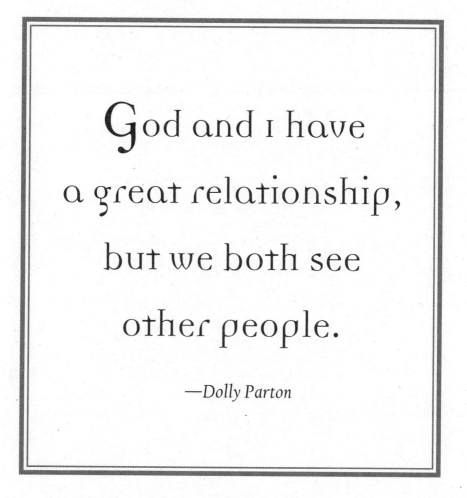

God and I have
a great relationship,
but we both see
other people.

—*Dolly Parton*

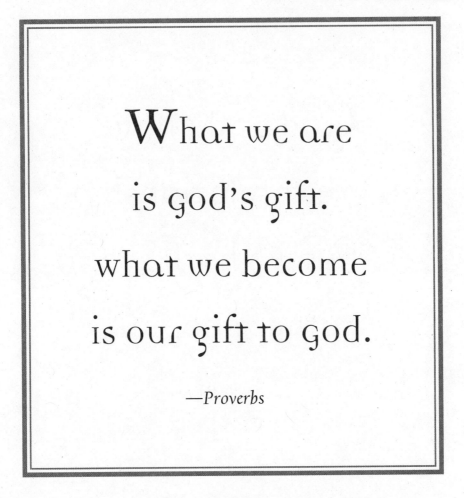

What we are is god's gift.

what we become is our gift to god.

—*Proverbs*

Start small.

Bless one moment

for what it brings you.

Say one ancient prayer.

Link yourself with continuity

& eternity. Fill one silence with

your end of the conversation.

No one can do this for you.

It belongs to you.

—*High Holiday Message*

glossary

Al chait	Traditional prayer of forgiveness
Aliyah	To ascend, to go up to the Torah
Ayn Keloheinu	Well known Jewish hymn
Ba-al Tekiah	Shofar player
Bima	Reader's stand in the synagogue
Bubbe	Grandmother
Cantor	Synagogue's music leader
Challah	Special bread for Shabbat and festivals
Chutzpah	Nerve, guts
Davening	Another word for praying plate
Days of Awe	Days between Rosh Hashanah and Yom Kippur
Erev	Night before a holiday
Gefilte fish	Mixture of chopped fish
Haftorah	Selection from the prophets

Hallel	Seasonal blessing
Hamotzi	Blessing over the bread
Havura	A group that prays and studies together
Hazzan	Other word for Cantor
Kiddush	Blessing over wine
Kippot	Plural of yarmulke, head covering
Kol Nidre	Prayer chanted on Yom Kippur
Kreplach	Meat-filled dough served in chicken soup
Kugel	Noodle or potato dish
Litvisher shul	People from an area in Russia
MaTovu	Song welcoming the Sabbath
Matzah balls	Balls cooked with matzah meal and eggs and served in soup
Minyan	Number of people required for religious service
Munach	One of the musical notes
Neilah service	Final service on Yom Kippur
Nusach	Cantorial motife used in prayer

Oneg	Social time after service
Pareve	Neither a meat product nor dairy
Rosh Hashanah	Jewish New Year
Rugelach	A rolled, sweet pastry
Schecter girls	Girls who attend Solomon Schecter Day School
Shabbat	Sabbath, day of rest
Shabbat Shuvah	Shabbat of Repentance, between Rosh Hashanah and Yom Kippur
Seder	Ceremony and dinner on the first nights of Passover
Shabbaton	Weekend of Shabbat activities
Shacharit service	Prayers recited in the morning
Shalom	Hello or peace or good-by
Shir HaShirim	Song of Songs
Shofar	Ram's horn, blown as a call to worship
Shul	Other name for synagogue
Sukkot	Feast of Tabernacles

Tallit	Prayer shawl
Talmud	Torah commentaries
Tashlich	"Casting off" your sins, traditionally by throwing bits of bread into a body of flowing water
Torah	First five books of the Hebrew Bible
Trope	Musical notes
Tszimmes	A mixture of food, usually carrots, prunes, and meat
Yarmulke	Head covering
Yarsheit candle	Candle that is lit on the anniversary of a death
Yiskor	A day to remember people who are no longer living
Yom Kippur	Day of Atonement
Yom Tov	Another term for High Holidays
Yontiff	Yiddish for any Jewish holiday
Zayde	Grandfather

acknowledgements

No book is done alone and especially not this one. I offer my sincere appreciation to the many people who told me their High Holiday memories. Special thanks go to Micaela Hellman-Tincher, Gerald M. Siegel, Rabbi Barbara Aiello, (www.rabbibarbara.com), Jack Engel, Kiera Elizabeth Wiatrak, Daily Cardinal, Jason Rubin, (www.jewsingreen.com), Josh Lapowsky, New Jersey Standard, Raphael Kadushin, Epicurious, Kiera Elizabeth Wiatrak, and Georgie Tarn and Tracey Fine (www.thejewishprincess.com).

To Don Lessne, I appreciate the fine opportunity you gave me. And to Elena Solis, the only person who works as many hours as I do, you made the book a work of art!

To my family, my brother Dick, my sister Janie, and the best twin brother ever, Tom, thanks for sharing all of my real life High Holidays at our house on 53rd and Farnam Street.

But most of all, I am still thankful to have the two finest daughters anyone could wish for: Amy Levine and Wendy Katzman. I hope they will create a lifetime of their own High Holiday stories.

A portion of the profits
from this book are being donated to
The Kripke Federation Jewish Library
in Omaha, Nebraska.